MW00805791

Pastoral and Spiritual
Care in a Digital Age

Emerging Perspectives in Pastoral Theology and Care

Series Editor: Kirk A. Bingaman, Fordham University

The field of pastoral care and counseling, and by extension pastoral theology, is presently at a crossroads, in urgent need of redefining itself for the age of postmodernity or even post-postmodernity. While there is, to be sure, a rich historical foundation upon which the field can build, it remains for contemporary scholars, educators, and practitioners to chart new directions for the present day and age. Emerging Perspectives in Pastoral Theology and Care seeks to meet this pressing need by inviting researchers in the field to address timely issues, such as the findings of contemplative neuroscience, the impact of technology on human development and wellness, mindfulness meditation practice for reducing anxiety, trauma viewed through the lens of positive psychology and resilience theory, clergy health and wellness, postmodern and multicultural pastoral care and counseling, and issues of race and class. The series will therefore serve as an important and foundational resource for years to come, guiding scholars and educators in the field in developing more contemporary models of theory and practice.

Titles in the Series

Pastoral and Spiritual Care in a Digital Age

The Future Is Now

Kirk A. Bingaman

LEXINGTON BOOKS
Lanham • Boulder • New York • London

Published by Lexington Books
An imprint of The Rowman & Littlefield Publishing Group, Inc.
4501 Forbes Boulevard, Suite 200, Lanham, Maryland 20706
www.rowman.com

6 Tinworth Street, London SE11 5AL, United Kingdom

Copyright © 2018 by The Rowman & Littlefield Publishing Group, Inc.

All rights reserved. No part of this book may be reproduced in any form or by any electronic or mechanical means, including information storage and retrieval systems, without written permission from the publisher, except by a reviewer who may quote passages in a review.

British Library Cataloguing in Publication Information Available

Library of Congress Cataloging-in-Publication Data Available

ISBN 978-1-4985-5341-4 (cloth : alk. paper)
ISBN 978-1-4985-5342-1 (electronic)

∞™ The paper used in this publication meets the minimum requirements of American National Standard for Information Sciences Permanence of Paper for Printed Library Materials, ANSI/NISO Z39.48-1992.

Printed in the United States of America

Contents

Acknowledgments

I am grateful for the support of so many colleagues, friends, and family the past two years, particularly with a project that has taken me into a whole new world of research, focusing on the rapid advance of digital technologies and artificial intelligence (AI) and how it is changing everything, including us. To say that even in just two years it has at times been challenging to keep up with the *speed* of the advance, and the perpetual new developments in the field of machine learning, would be an understatement. My deep concern is for those of us on the front lines of caring for anxious clients, students, congregants, and faith communities, for ourselves in the midst of what is at bottom unprecedented change. I thank the staff of Lexington Books for their support of the book series I am editing, *Emerging Perspectives in Pastoral Theology and Care*, which includes this book project. Having worked with Lexington before on an earlier book (*The Power of Neuroplasticity for Pastoral and Spiritual Care*, 2014), I have experienced firsthand a high level of quality and professionalism. Specifically, I thank the acquisition editors that I have worked with these two years, Michael Gibson, Judith Lakamper, and Sarah Craig, as well as my production editor, Paula Williamson. And, to Drs. Ilia Delio, Carrie Doehring, and Ted Peters, I cannot thank you enough for your generous endorsements.

Fordham University and its Office of Research awarded me a faculty fellowship and sabbatical to work on the project, which gave me the necessary time to see it through to completion. I am grateful to the Graduate School of Religion and Religious Education (GSRRE) at Fordham, to my dean, Fr. Faustino (Tito) Cruz, S.M., for his generous support, along with the GSRRE faculty and staff, including my pastoral care and counseling faculty colleagues, Drs. Lisa Cataldo and Mary Beth Werdel. I also thank my faculty colleague, Fr. Francis (Frank) McAloon, S.J., for the helpful conversations about the theology of Karl Rahner. In the Office of Research at Fordham, I thank Dr. Z. George Hong, Chief Research Officer, and Celinett Rodriguez, grant officer, for their support and interest in the research. The project began taking shape over the course of the past few years in the context of the New Directions in Pastoral Theology Group at Princeton Theological Seminary. I thank my colleagues in the group for their support of the "new direction" of my research, into a realm that before I never would have imagined. To Dr. Jaco Hamman, thank you for also taking a similar direction with your research, and for the discussions we have had about the proliferation of digital technologies.

I thank staff and colleagues at the Lutheran Counseling Center of New York, for their curiosity about the project, including executive director Molly Blancke and office manager Rosemary Kerrane. And, to the Scarborough Presbyterian Church in Scarborough, NY, where I have shared my research interests from the pulpit and at coffee hour, thank you for your interest and support. To the Rev. Dr. Tim Ives and Elder Jeff Jahier, thank you for the many in-depth conversations about the advance of AI and its impact on us, and where God might be in the midst of it all. I thank Patricia Williams, LCSW, for her accompaniment along the way, and for the ongoing support and thoughtful reflection. I am grateful to the Tergar Meditation Community at Graymoor Spiritual Life Center in Garrison NY, and to meditation teacher Joy Baum, for the contemplative-meditational practice both at Graymoor and along the Hudson River at sunset. Thank you to my parents and to my brother, Brad, not only for your support but also for your curiosity about AI and the theological implications. To my daughter Annie, thank you for your commitment, personal and professional, to making the world a better place, and to helping guide the momentous change toward more hopeful ends. Finally, to the people of the Dolpo region of northwestern Nepal, whom I met along the way in my Himalayan trek, thank you for showing me firsthand the importance of living mindfully in the present moment, even while increasing in such a remote location your technological intelligence.

Introduction

*Pastoral and Spiritual Care in a
Digital Age: The Future is Now*

INTRODUCTION

Human beings have entered an era of unprecedented change, reflected in the rapid and sophisticated advances in technology, digital speed, and computer processing power. Indeed, at the present moment we are "riding on a curve of dramatically increasing complexity . . . we need only extrapolate the technological portion of the curve a little way into the future to reach an important tipping point" (Shanahan, 2015, p. xix). The "tipping point" is the moment when we arrive at what has become known as the "technological singularity," when machine intelligence approaches and eventually merges with our own human intelligence, or when technology merges with human biology. There is of course considerable debate about the nature and the timing of the singularity, the precise moment when it will become a tangible reality. Estimates vary from as soon as thirty years from now, i.e., by or before the middle of the century, to maybe the end of this century or early next century. It all depends on how fast technology continues to evolve, which at its present rate already seems to be approaching light speed. Compare this to the rate of biological change and evolution, which is obviously a much slower process, most often at a proverbial snail's pace, and we can see without too much difficulty a distinct possibility for the singularity's occurrence in the not-too-distant future. Perhaps it is the speed with which technology is advancing that is most compelling, when we stop to consider that the smartphone we use today has "more computer power than *all* of NASA when it put two [astronauts] on the moon in 1969" (Kaku, 2014, p. 9). The growing consensus in the scientific community is that it is not a matter of *if* machine intelligence will eventually merge with and then surpass human intelligence, but inevitably *how* and *when*. When it does occur, whether in thirty or fifty or a hundred years or longer, the effects will be seismic for the human individual and for human society, with important and rather obvious implications for pastoral and spiritual care. As Murray Shanahan (2015) has noted, working in the field of cognitive robotics at Imperial College in London, "There is no need to lay down a timetable for progress in artificial intelligence, or to pinpoint a date for the arrival of superintelligence, in order to see that AI technology has the potential to reshape human society within a few generations" (p. 163).

Whether the technological singularity, which would signal an unprecedented leap forward in terms of human evolution, occurs sooner or later, the fact is that "we are already in the midst of a major evolutionary transition that merges technology, biology, and society" (Gillings *et al.*, 2016, p. 11). To be sure, human life in the Western world, and increasingly the world over, occurs more and more on the "screen," to use Sherry Turkle's (1995) word. "From a social perspective, digital technology has infiltrated the fabric of human society to a degree of undisputable and often life-sustaining dependence" (Gillings *et al.*, 2016, p. 11). One can therefore argue that we are now beyond the point of no return, that technology has become and will continue to be central to the whole evolutionary process, moving us forward into an uncharted era of human and cognitive enhancement. Even now research is revealing that the human brain has already undergone technological enhancement and modification, from life on the technological screen, and that the merger of technology with human intelligence is already underway. Our neural pathways are being rerouted in very specific ways by our increasing reliance on technology, to the extent that certain neural regions and cognitive skills are strengthened and enhanced while other areas of the brain, and the skills associated with those areas, see less activity and development.

For example, there is evidence that as we spend more and more time online, the *average individual*, and not only the video gamer, experiences neural enhancement by way of greater processing speed, faster problem-solving skills, the ability to size up information and situations more rapidly, and improvements in visuomotor and visual-spatial coordination. We know from neuroscientific studies that neurons that continually fire together will begin wiring together with greater strength and force (Siegel, 2011, p. 148), so it is understandable that as we fire more and more often the neurons associated with processing speed, problem-solving capacity, and visual-spatial coordination those neural groupings will become stronger and stronger. At the same time, neural groupings that we fire less often in our increased time on the screen, such as those associated with attentional control, relational intelligence, and a deeper mindful and contemplative awareness, are wiring together with less strength and force, perhaps even weakening. "Given our brain's plasticity, we know that our online habits continue to reverberate in the workings of our synapses when we are not online," so that "neural circuits devoted to scanning, skimming, and multitasking are expanding and strengthening, while those used for reading and thinking deeply, with sustained concentration, are weakening or eroding" (Carr, 2010, p. 141).

Lest it appear that I am about to take the situation-is-dire path with this book, I want to be clear that my hope is to put forward a more evenhanded assessment of the current milieu, with its unique challenges *and* opportunities for pastoral, spiritual, and clinical practitioners and for those in our care. Methodologically, then, I will be following to a certain extent the correlational method of inquiry, in keeping with Paul Tillich's (1973) approach, in which religious and theological knowledge and experience is held in dialectical and dialogical tension with the findings of science in general and those of cognitive neuroscience in particular. Moreover, the method of correlation is also a useful framework for holding both the opportunities and challenges of the present digital age in dialectical tension, the hopes and fears as I intend to do, without resorting to an all-good or all-bad assessment of technological enhancement. Beyond a correlational method of inquiry, however, which would support a healthy *dialogue* between very different fields and disciplines, e.g., theology and science, and between very different views of the current situation, e.g., the potential benefits of rapid technological progress and the potential threats, I will attempt to offer an approach that goes beyond mere dialogue toward that of *integration*, in keeping with Ian Barbour's (1997) groundbreaking work in the area of religion and science. Barbour (1997) has noted that he is "open to an extension of what are taken to be the boundaries of acceptable science and religion and to the possibility of new paradigms that are more inclusive" (p. 98). Certainly, if we are on the threshold of unprecedented change and an unprecedented evolutionary leap forward, then we will need more than ever new integrative paradigms for guiding the work of pastoral and spiritual care, paradigms that have the capacity to evenhandedly hold *both* our narratives of hope and wonder *and* other narratives of apprehension and fear:

> The presence of narratives of hope does not—and should not—eliminate the narratives of apprehension present within contemporary technoculture. Hope arises from theological reflection of the tension between wonder and anxiety, as each informs the other, and drives to the fore essential questions about human technological agency. It is essential to have avenues—in communities of faith, in the academy, and in the public square—for raising, discussing, and answering these questions so as to provide hope in the face of this tension between awe and anxiety. Narratives of hope do not displace those of apprehension but rather exist in symbiosis, which allows apprehension to serve a positive purpose in society. (Garner, 2011, p. 98)

As the so-called "singularity" approaches in coming years and decades, technology will increasingly catch up with and begin to match human intelligence, which as we know only too well evolves at a significantly slower rate. Whenever the moment occurs in the future, the effects will again be seismic and will represent a revolutionary leap forward in the human evolutionary process. The implications for pastoral and spiritual care, for clinical practice, and for pastoral and practical theology are significant, for the current situation necessitates immediate theological reflection about human nature and what constitutes human personhood in a digital age of increased technological enhancement and modification. For example, who or what are we becoming as human individuals, as a human race, as a human species, with technology becoming more and more an integral force in our development and evolution? As Ilia Delio (2008) has noted, "The integration of technology in human life is of such degree that we must now consider the possibility of being techno-sapiens" (p. 13). This is a startling statement, to be sure, and yet it is not without mounting evidence revealing that human beings are presently going through a profound shift in evolution and identity. From extensive studies at the Brain Research Institute at UCLA, Gary Small has found that "the current explosion of digital technology not only is changing the way we live and communicate but is rapidly and profoundly altering our brains" (Small & Vorgan, 2008, p. 1). If in fact human beings have begun the evolutionary transition from being Homo sapiens to increasingly Techno sapiens, then again this necessitates *immediate* theological reflection about what constitutes human development and nature in the present and in the future. Moreover, what are the implications for a theology of *Imago Dei*, central to the practice of pastoral and spiritual care? Are technologically enhanced human individuals or even Techno sapiens still created *Imago Dei*, at least in the way the doctrine and theology has been understood and put forward historically? It would seem that from a theological position, "it is necessary to determine whether human-technology integration is able to meet the conditions that safeguard the sanctity of the person who is the 'image of God' (*Imago Dei*)" (Fisher, 2015, p. 27).

More immediately, the pressing issue is helping those in our care develop greater attentional control and mindful awareness, in order to be less at the mercy of the digital bombardment. As we know, neuroplasticity can work both ways, either in the direction of greater health and well-being or in the opposite direction, as neural regions associated with anxious awareness become strengthened and more ingrained over time. We can be certain that neurons that we continue to fire together, whether or not we are always conscious of what we are doing, will wire together with energy and force over time, until a new neural baseline or a new "normal" emerges, for better or in other cases for worse. "As particular circuits in our brain strengthen through the repetition of physical or mental activity, they begin to transform the activity into a habit" (Carr, 2010, p. 34). Increased time on the screen or on the Net, as I noted earlier, strengthens circuitry associated with neural processing speed, problem solving, and eye-hand coordination, for the neurons that we are firing repetitively through our digital activities support these particular skills until they become as it were "hardwired," imperceptively establishing a new baseline in the brain. But the new baseline or new "normal" for today's digital world is, like anything else, rather double-edged, for while it can certainly be advantageous to develop faster processing speeds and problem-solving skills, we are learning that the downside is a decreasing rate of sustained focus and concentration.

To state the obvious, the human brain can be on overload as it attempts to process the unrelenting flow of information that comes our way in today's digital world. As we attempt to focus on one item of information, whether it be a breaking news story, an update about the financial markets, or something that needs our undivided attention at work, we are simultaneously bombarded with other information that seemingly needs our immediate attention too. We therefore fire up neural regions associated with the skills of higher processing speed and so-called multitasking, trying to meet the cultural expectation to keep up with it all. And yet, neural regions associated with sustained focus and attentional control, strengthened through what the neuroscientist would call the practice of one-pointed concentration, get neglected in this illusory pursuit. It is very important to keep in mind that the brain we have today is remarkably similar and almost identical to the "stone-age brain" of thousands of years ago, with one obvious caveat: "The same brain now has to take on the torrent of information that the digital society discharges over us" (Klingberg, 2009, pp. 10–11).

Neurons that we consciously and/or unconsciously fire together repeatedly will over time wire together more robustly, so that neural regions associated with faster processing of the digital information are gaining in strength. At the same time, other circuitry fundamental to human experience for centuries and millennia, such as that supporting the capacity for attentional depth, contemplative living, and relational and compassionate awareness, is activated less often, with a gradual weakening of these neural pathways. Human identity, particularly what makes us uniquely human, has the potential to be fundamentally altered in the matter of a few decades, unless we find a way to mindfully keep ourselves grounded and centered in contemplative awareness and living. This will require the intentional and sustained activation of neurons in other regions of the brain, specifically those supporting the human attentional capacity. To a certain extent, we and those in our care still have a choice, even if the choice to live more mindfully and contemplatively, to cultivate greater attentional control, is not supported by the present digital culture. We still have a measure of control, even in the midst of the digital bombardment, which in many ways is fundamentally a narrative of hope.

That said, pastoral and spiritual care in the coming years, our own self-care as well, will not be easy, for it will require a more focused attention to and cultivation of the neural circuitry that is increasingly neglected in today's digital world. As Nicholas Carr (2010) reminds us:

> What we are *not* doing when we are online also has neurological conse-quences. Just as neurons that fire together wire together, neurons that do not fire together do not wire together. As the time we spend scanning Web pages crowds out the time we spend reading books, as the time we spend exchanging bite-sized text messages crowds out the time we spend composing sentences and paragraphs, as the time we spend hopping across links crowds out the time we devote to quiet reflection and contemplation, the circuits that support those old intellectual functions and pursuits weaken and begin to break apart. The brain recycles the disused neurons and synapses for other, more pressing work. We gain new skills and perspectives but lose old ones. (p. 120)

In an earlier publication (Bingaman, 2014), I discussed the importance of contemplative-meditational practice for the work of pastoral and spiritual care, specifically for helping clients and congregants lower stress, reduce anxious awareness, and live more mindfully in the peace and joy of the present moment. I even went so far as to argue for a paradigm shift in religious communities, where in these anxious times we begin elevating con-templative spiritual practice to a place of comparable importance with relig-ious belief and doctrine. Building on this theme, I want to continue to empha-size the central importance of regular contemplative-meditational practice for practitioners and for those in our care, albeit with a slightly different twist in the context of this particular study. There are, to be sure, definitive studies revealing that the regular practice of mindfulness meditation and/or contem-plative prayer has the capacity to lower activity in the limbic area or the stress and arousal region of the brain (e.g., Lazar, 2013b), even while simul-taneously increasing the higher-order activity and executive functioning of the prefrontal cortex, a neural region vital for self-regulation. The findings have important implications for this study, in terms of how we go about self-regulating in a frenetic digital world, and how we can intentionally and regularly fire the neural circuitry connected to attentional control and mind-ful awareness so that it hardwires accordingly. "If we look more closely at the scientific literature, we can find a whole host of studies than can be interpreted in the same way as ours: namely, that working memory and the control of attention can be trained" (Klingberg, 2009, p. 123). While there are more than a few cognitive therapeutic techniques that focus on the build-ing up of our "attention muscle," I would argue that contemplative-medita-tional practice, a core feature of recent mindfulness-based cognitive thera-pies, naturally and quintessentially lends itself to this work in the context of pastoral and spiritual care. The regular practice of contemplative prayer, for example, has the capacity over time to calm the anxious brain, as we are learning from the emerging field of contemplative neuroscience. Additionally, it can also be of great benefit when it comes to increasing our attentional control and self-regulation, as we learn to manage the perpetual torrent of information and its impact on our overall health and well-being.

We know that the practice of contemplative prayer and meditation has been at the disposal of pastoral and spiritual care providers for quite some time now, centuries and even millennia, only now we know that above and beyond the spiritual benefits of regular contemplative practice there are other benefits too, including the psycho-physiological benefit of rewiring the brain's neural pathways. As Daniel Siegel (2007) points out, centering ourselves contemplatively in the present moment of our lived experience, whether through regular spiritual practice and/or mindfulness meditation, "offers a powerful path toward both compassion and inner well-being," for it is what neuroscience now verifies *and* what has already been taught over thousands of years of religious and spiritual practice (p. 96). Moreover, pastoral and spiritual care providers have at their disposal mindfulness-based therapeutic frameworks for guiding their work with clients and congregants, contemporary approaches that make contemplative-meditational practice a core focus of the therapy. Mindfulness-based therapies, which are included in the recent third-wave of cognitive therapeutic approaches, very intentionally use meditational practice, both within and outside the therapy session, to help clients increase attentional stability and metacognitive awareness. Attentional control and stability, or the self-regulation of attention, is for example a central feature and goal of Mindfulness-Based Cognitive Therapy (MBCT), for "intentionally focusing undivided attention on thoughts, emotions, and sensations in this way uses much of the individual's capacity for attentional processing, so that little capacity remains for rumination" (Coffman *et al.*, 2006, p. 34). The practice of attentional regulation follows closely the neuroscientific research that "examines the neural bases of mood and emotion" (Fresco *et al.*, 2011, pp. 57–58), and the neural regions that support sustained concentration and mindful awareness.

The remainder of the book will be devoted to exploring these and other issues in greater depth and detail, in the interest of putting forward an approach to pastoral and spiritual care and to clinical practice that can be contextualized for the present digital age. This presupposes a very precise understanding of the current "landscape," of the rapid and extraordinary advance of computer science and machine intelligence in recent years, and technology's increasingly dominant role in the evolutionary process and more specifically in human evolution, which will be the focus of chapter 1. The evolutionary changes will be even more dramatic and seismic as we approach the technological singularity, in whatever shape or form, when we witness and experience a more complete merger of biology with technology, of our own human intelligence with machine learning. When it occurs, it will not be long before artificial intelligence (AI) surpasses us, given the dramatic differential between the rate of evolutionary change for technology compared to that of our own human biology. The challenge if not problem, as Ilia Delio (2008) puts it rather concisely, is now the accelerated rate of evolutionary advance, which, "as the specialists of technology indicate, is running faster than the human intellect can comprehend because of the ingenuity and crea-tivity of humans themselves" (p. 178). What is important to keep in mind, for pastoral, spiritual, and clinical practitioners, is that technology has become the primary driving force guiding the evolutionary process, and that clients and congregants in our care, we ourselves are now more technologically dependent than we sometimes realize. "The integration of technology in daily human life around the globe has rendered us technologically dependent human beings for whom technology organizes contemporary life" (Delio, 2008, pp. 162–163). The obvious question is, how far can it go? We will attempt to answer this important and timely question, in a way that focuses more on scientific fact than on science fiction.

Theological narratives focusing on the age of technology are beginning to emerge, ranging from awe and wonder to fear and apprehension. If we are in fact on the way to becoming, at the very least, technologically enhanced human beings, if not Techno sapiens in coming decades, then the current situation calls for immediate theological reflection. In chapter 2, I will be looking to Karl Rahner (1978), and specifically to his theology of *Vorgriff*, as a way to help us frame the unique challenges of the present day and age. For Rahner (1978), the human individual is "a transcendent being insofar as all of his [sic] knowledge and all of his conscious activity is grounded in a pre-apprehension (*Vorgriff*) of 'being' as such, in an unthematic but ever-present knowledge of the infinity of reality" (p. 33). The human person, as well as human nature for that matter, is fundamentally evolutionary for Rahner (1969), perpetually in a state of becoming and emergence. Accordingly, "it is a *capacity* of dynamic self-movement of the spirit, given *a priori* with human nature, directed towards all possible objects" (p. 59). This dynamic self-movement and openness directed toward *all* possible objects would include technology, with the possibility of becoming more than we have ever been before as human beings. Because the human relation to God is framed by way of a theology of hope and perpetual becoming, the *Vorgriff* is "portrayed dynamically as a reaching-out for God . . . a movement not just to God, but also to the future—in fact, Rahner seems to equate the two" (Ludlow, 2000, p. 126).

All of this has relevance for the matter of human nature, the focus of chapter 3, and what ultimately will constitute human personhood in a very different digital world. For example, how will we view technologically en-hanced human individuals, clients and congregants in our pastoral and spiritual care, from the standpoint of a theology of *Imago Dei*? How will we understand *Imago Dei* in light of the coming merger of humans with machines, perhaps even the emergence of Techno sapiens or some other equivalent, which could very well represent something in the way of a "new being" in the evolutionary process? I will argue that Rahner's (1978) theology of *Vorgriff*, his focus on a pre-apprehension of infinite mystery and reality and an emerging grasp of what potentially lies ahead of us, will give us a useful *and* a hopeful framework in which to situate our theological reflection of human nature, present and future. As Rahner has said,

> Evolutionary change occurs because of a power that comes from within the creature—the pressure of the divine acting from within. He identified this pressure from within as God who is the heart of evolutionary change, as a power that enables the creature to go beyond itself and become more than it was. (Delio, 2008, p. 75)

Pre-apprehension of what lies ahead, a grasp of what is about to emerge in coming years and decades, assumes the capacity, individually and collectively, for attentional focus and reflective awareness. However, the digital culture does not support us in cultivating mindful and contemplative living, and we can expect that it will support it even less in the future with the accelerating rate of technological advance. Preparatory to cultivating a deeper mindful and contemplative awareness is learning to sustain one's attention, to develop the capacity for attentional control and stability, which I will be discussing in chapter 4. But attentional stability does not come easily in a digital world, where the expectation is to cognitively process more and more information simultaneously, faster and faster. "Life on the screen" does contribute to higher rates of neural processing speed, and to more rapid problem-solving, which is certainly advantageous for people of all ages. That said, studies also reveal a more sobering finding, that sustained attention and concentration, along with the capacity for in-depth reflection and introspective processing, fundamental to human nature and experience for millennia, is declining. There are ways, however, to activate and strengthen the neural circuitry supporting the development of sustained attention and reflection, most notably through regular contemplative-meditational practice, the focus of chapter 5. Neurons that we intentionally fire together on a regular basis will wire together with greater strength and force, so that in our contemplative spiritual practice we are continually firing and wiring specific neural regions that support attentional control, higher-order thinking, self-regulation, and compassionate awareness. It is important that pastoral and spiritual practitioners, that clergy and faith communities grasp the urgency of the matter, that we begin elevating contemplative-meditational practice to a level of comparable importance with religious belief and church teaching and doctrine, lest the opportunity to preserve what has been unique to human identity and spirituality passes us by.

It should be clear that I intend to take something of a "middle path" with this study, between the extremes of technology viewed as either an all-good or an all-bad object. On the one hand, there are significant risks involved as we move further and further into an age of increased technological enhancement, risks to what has made us uniquely human and uniquely *Imago Dei* for millennia. On the other hand, it is not wise to support a quasi-Luddite stance, where the approach to technology and technological progress is exclusively oppositional. This extreme view does not fully grasp the current situation, with technology becoming more and more the dominant organizing force in the evolutionary process, or maybe it does, albeit it in a reactionary and defiant way. There is mounting evidence that we are already well into an unprecedented evolutionary leap forward, and that it will take sustained and in-depth theological reflection to create frames of reference geared toward effective pastoral and spiritual care in a digital age. "It cannot be merely a religious way of dealing with technology, as if it were external to who we are; rather, technology has become part and parcel of who we are" (Delio, 2008, pp. 163–164). To be sure, those in our care, and we ourselves, have now taken to life on the screen in earnest, and help is needed to navigate the complex terrain that is ahead of us. Toward that end, in chapter 6 I will be formulating an approach to pastoral and spiritual care and clinical practice that intentionally engages the current situation and reality by way of mindfulness-based therapy. This particular therapeutic framework has the distinct advantage of helping us cultivate greater attentional focus and sustained concentration, necessary for developing an informed understanding of and effective response to the pressing exigencies of a digital age.

Chapter One

The Rapid Advance and Proliferation of Digital Technologies

Toward the end of *Homo Deus: A Brief History of Tomorrow*, the sequel to his best-selling book, *Sapiens: A Brief History of Humanity*, the historian Yuval Noah Harari (2017) writes, "from a historical perspective it is clear that something momentous is happening" (p. 370). Our present environment is changing in such extraordinary ways, has *already* changed dramatically in response to the rapid advance of technology, so much so that we are nearing a pivotal tipping point in human history. In a matter of a few decades, we have witnessed researchers in the field of technology and artificial intelligence (AI) turn "a limited breakthrough in computer science into a world-shattering cataclysm that may completely transform the very nature of life" (Harari, 2017, p. 373). What began as a limited breakthrough in computer science and computational processing has now developed at an accelerated rate into the proliferation of machine intelligence, which increasingly pervades the entire spectrum of human life. Indeed, from all indications, it appears as if we have passed beyond one tipping point already, with our everyday dependence on the electronic "screen." Think of our growing reliance on social media and social networking, and on the algorithmic precision of our so-called "personal digital assistants," who seemingly wait to respond to our commands and questions with an uncanny immediacy. "Whether at home or away, inside or out, we have Siri, Alexa . . . who are becoming increasingly useful, but also increasingly ubiquitous" (Hendler & Mulvehill, 2016, p. 3). Perhaps hard to even imagine, this is only the beginning of what is awaiting us, as we get closer and closer to a more dramatic and momentous tipping point: the eventual merger of machine intelligence with human intelligence, what some refer to as the technological singularity. In many ways, we have crossed the point of no return, with technology becoming ever

1

important in the evolutionary process, superseding biology as the primary organizing force in the present digital milieu. For some of us, this will take some getting used to, learning to accept that even if we wanted to, there is no turning back. The reality of technology and artificial intelligence is here to stay; in fact, we can even say that this particular "train," so to speak, has already left the station. Given the centrality of technology in the current evolutionary process, it is important to remember that even if we could somehow manage to "hit the brakes" with further technological advances, "our economy will collapse, along with our society" (Harari, 2017, p. 51).

AN EVER-INCREASING RATE OF SPEED

What has been most surprising about the extraordinary leap in technological growth and progress is not that machine intelligence has been gaining on us, that it continues to make strides in the quest to catch up with human intelligence, but rather the current *speed* with which it is doing so. Those on the front lines of the scientific research have been fairly confident that machine learning would continue to grow and evolve in coming years, and that someday on the distant horizon it could approximate and perhaps even overtake human cognition. Increasingly, however, it appears that if artificial intelligence continues to develop at its present accelerated rate, it will have the capacity to match and overtake us sooner than was expected, in a matter of decades rather than centuries. Harari (2017) points out that "scientific research and technological developments are moving at a far faster rate than most of us can grasp" (p. 50), a dizzying rate in fact if one attempts to keep up with all the stunning breakthroughs. But Harari (2017) is hardly alone in conveying a sense of wonderment and surprise at the speed with which technology and artificial intelligence is presently evolving. Nick Bostrom (2016), for example, in his bestselling book, *Superintelligence: Paths, Dangers, Strategies*, similarly notes that "technical progress in machine learning has been swifter than most had expected" (p. 321), driven in large measure by the advances in what is known as "deep (artificial) neural networks" and the related field of "deep learning." Thanks to a combination of faster computers, larger data sets, and algorithmic refinements, "deep learning methods—essentially many-layered neural networks—have begun to approach (and in some cases exceed) human performance on many perceptual tasks, including handwriting recognition, image recognition and image captioning, speech recognition, and facial recognition" (Bostrom, 2016, p. 321). The renowned filmmaker, Werner Herzog (2016), has also expressed a sense of awe and wonder at the speed of artificial-intelligence research. Reflecting on his acclaimed and compelling documentary, *Lo and Behold*, Reveries of the Connected World, which focuses on the evolution of the Internet, he comments, "I am not surprised by how far [the field of artificial intelligence] has come, but I am surprised by the speed with which it has come upon us." Even the experts themselves, who are doing the research in the field of artificial intelligence, express the same feeling of awe and wonder, as well as a feeling of uneasiness. As James Hendler and Alice Mulvehill (2016) have noted, near the end of their important book, *Social Machines: The Coming Collision of Artificial Intelligence, Social Networking, and Humanity*, "The speed with which this technology is moving is also unsettling:"

> When we started writing this book, we discussed why it would be really hard for an AI system to ever beat a human at the game of Go. At our first rewrite, we had to update that chapter to say that new technologies were making it possible that a computer might be reaching human-level play. Before the page proofs came, we were rewriting again to talk about AlphaGo's feat in beating one of the best human players. (p. 166)

AlphaGo was developed by Google's DeepMind AI to outperform the best human player at the game of Go, a complicated board game that origi- nated in China thousands of years ago, which it finally did in March 2016. It is considered by many to be an evolutionary leap forward in the development of AI, an important sign of what is potentially looming on the not-too-distant horizon. Currently, the field of AI is in the "artificial *narrow* intelligence" (ANI) or weak AI stage, with machine intelligence capable of outperforming human beings at a single task or in one area. AlphaGo's victory over the best Go player in the world, and subsequent wins over other human Go players of near equal rank, is a prime example of the accelerating development of ANI. Years before AlphaGo, there was IBM's Deep Blue, which of course paved the way for the advancement of ANI with its groundbreaking victory over the reigning world chess champion, followed by Watson's well-publicized win- ning performance on the television game show, *Jeopardy*. These are but a few examples of artificial *narrow* intelligence, for it is becoming increasing- ly apparent that the number of "single tasks" that machine intelligence can outperform human intelligence is on the steady rise. Other examples include the reliance of car mechanics and airline pilots on computer intelligence, our own everyday reliance on the superior intelligence of the smartphone, with its computer-generated digital assistant (Siri), navigation system (GPS), and tailor-made recommendations for our music and shopping enjoyment. Addi- tionally, ANI has made great inroads in outperforming humans in the world of healthcare and finance, respectively in helping medical practitioners with greater diagnostic precision and with the emergence of sophisticated algo- rithmic trading for investment strategists. For example, "in a recent experi- ment a computer algorithm correctly diagnosed ninety percent of lung cancer cases presented to it, while human doctors had a success rate of only fifty percent" (Harari, 2017, p. 319).

As machine intelligence continues to outperform human intelligence with more and more of these singular tasks, there is growing concern that eventually it is going to coalesce into a more integrated phenomenon, when it reaches what is known as "artificial *general* intelligence" (AGI) or the strong AI stage, a human-level intelligence that can consistently perform most cognitive or intellectual tasks as well as any human being. When this occurs, make no mistake, it will be a significant "game changer," for we will then be *past* the tipping point and into a vastly different world. But this will not be the only game changer, or even the most significant one, for if and when AGI or human-level intelligence is achieved, artificial intelligence will continue to evolve with ever increasing speed onto the next stage, where it will become "superintelligent." Artificial *super*intelligence (ASI), or superhuman-level machine intelligence, can be defined "as any intellect that greatly exceeds the cognitive performance of humans in virtually all domains of interest" (Bostrom, 2016, p. 26). Its arrival would be nothing less than seismic, for in little or no time it would surpass us in all matters of interest, across the board, given its present rate of accelerated growth and change. We need only recall that already "within a short span of fifty years, computer-based technology has become the principal organizer of modern life" (Delio, 2013, p. 156), just to give us some idea of what is to come. What would have sounded not too long ago like it was completely out of the realm of science fiction, is rapidly becoming a more urgent topic for scientific researchers, technologists, ethicists, even for theologians as we will soon see. There is growing recognition across more and more fields and disciplines that something momentous is about to happen, has already started to happen, that what might have been science fiction years ago is now more and more within the realm of fact. For example, recent surveys of and interviews with the "experts" working on the front lines of artificial intelligence research reveal that it is not unreasonable to "believe that human-level machine intelligence has a fairly sizeable chance of being developed by mid-century," and "that it might perhaps fairly soon thereafter result in superintelligence" (Bostrom, 2016, p.25).

It is remarkable that as late as the 1990's, there was resounding critique that scientific researchers were wasting their time with artificial intelligence, that it amounted to little more than a pipedream (Hendler & Mulvehill, 2016, p. 6). Twenty years later, there is still plenty of criticism, only now it is the reverse of what it was before. In only two decades, "critics have gone from worrying that we were wasting our time to worrying that we will succeed, and possibly succeed too well . . . from arguing we should not pursue AI because it is impossible to arguing that we should not do AI because it is not" (Hendler & Mulvehill, 2016, p. 6). The theological implications, to state the obvious, are rather profound, as we move further and further into this uncharted territory at a far faster rate than many of us realize. But before we can have serious and in-depth theological reflection around the coming merger of humans and machines, we need to be very clear that we are keeping current scientific research separate from the science fiction of popular culture. For starters, we are *not* in a serious discussion of artificial intelligence talking about the Hollywood dramatics of the Terminator, as much as it has captivated our imagination, incredibly for more than thirty years spanning no less than five different film versions. And, there are reports that a sixth film is in the works, perhaps with Arnold Schwarzenegger even reprising his familiar role as the menacing cyborg. "Those inane Terminator pictures," argues Bostrom (2016), "are taking a toll," as they reinforce "misguided public alarm about evil robot armies" (p. 321). However, he adds, "away from the popular cacophony, it is now also possible—if one perks up one's ears and angles them correctly—to hear the low-key murmur of a more grownup conversation" (Bostrom, 2016, p. 321).

The "grownup conversation" and by extension serious theological reflection about the coming merger of humans and machines needs to immediately distinguish between the scientific research of the present from the sensationalism conveyed by science fiction and popular culture. This is not to say that robotic artificial intelligence, or cognitive robotics is not worthy of a robust conversation in its own right, notwithstanding the misguided popular cacophony. There could very well come a day when robotics "evolves" to the point of complete autonomy, without the need for human programmers, but in all likelihood this day will be well beyond the singularity and the human-machine merger. The technological singularity, therefore, will not be an "apocalyptic scenario" that emerges with great drama and fanfare, let alone with hordes of robotic armies. Rather, it will gradually come upon us, perhaps sooner rather than later, maybe even in a few decades, by way of "computational intelligence" and the sheer power of computer algorithms. The algorithms, writes Harari (2017), are not going to rise up and revolt and enslave us, but instead "will be so good at making decisions for us that it would be madness not to follow their advice" (p. 339). Thus, an important distinction to keep in mind, as we continue to reflect on the approaching technological singularity and the emergence of human-level machine learning, is between *robotic* artificial intelligence and *cognitive* artificial intelligence, the latter being more the focus of this book. "For many people," note Hendler and Mulvehill (2016), "when they think about artificial intelligence they immediately think (some fondly, some in fear) about mechanical humans who may someday live among us." They continue:

> That may or may not be, but without the cognitive aspects of AI to guide the robots' behaviors, they are like a human without a brain. . . . Without being powered by the technologies we discuss, robots would lurch around without aim, randomly interacting with people and things—not a pretty concept. We

absolutely agree that the technologies underlying the bodies and mechanics of robots are truly fascinating, and there are many books that can help you learn more about them, but our focus is on the coming revolution in cognitive AI: the part that thinks, not the part that moves. (p. 13)

The revolution in *cognitive* artificial intelligence is of course well underway, as we have been learning, as is our increasing merger with technology. What might have sounded a few years ago like something futuristic is already occurring, in everyday life and in daily mundane actions as "millions of people decide to grant their smartphone a bit more control over their lives" (Harari, 2017, p. 49). It is important to remember that even with the remarkable and revolutionary breakthroughs we have witnessed thus far in the development of machine intelligence and learning, it is only the beginning. The computational resources of the smartphone are still confined, at least for now, to the realm of artificial *narrow* intelligence (ANI), and to outperforming humans with singular tasks, such as navigation skills, healthcare decisions, financial management, and lifestyle choices generated by algorithmic feedback. That said, it is still worth remembering that even if it is *only* operational within the realm of ANI, the smartphone's present level of computational processing is extraordinary. The smartphone we use today, as we noted earlier, contains more computer power than *all* the computer power NASA had at its disposal when landing astronauts on the moon, a fact of no small importance. Additionally, the amount of memory on your phone "exceeds the total amount of memory storage that existed in the world in the late 1960s and early 1970s" (Hendler & Mulvehill, 2016, p. 46). Having it perpetually at our fingertips, consistently making use of it throughout the day, start to finish, and letting it think and make more and more decisions for us has in a matter of a few short years become second nature for millions of people. And little wonder too, for computer algorithms are already becoming so fast and sophisticated that it makes less and less sense not to follow their advice, as Harari (2017) suggested, and merely rely on our human intelligence alone. The human brain as we well know is an extraordinary information-processing system, containing upwards of around a hundred billion neurons, with considerable storage capacity. But at the same time the sobering reality is that the rate at which it accumulates information is very slow compared to how information is accumulated digitally. If we use the common measure for data storage capacity, i.e., the *bit*, "on one estimate, the adult human brain stores about one billion bits—a couple of orders of magnitude less than a low-end smartphone" (Bostrom, 2016, p. 73). Moreover, when it comes to comparing processing speeds, or the rate of processing information, "biological neurons operate at a peak speed of about 200 Hertz (Hz), a full seven orders of magnitude slower than a modern microprocessor (approximately 2 Gigahertz)" (Bostrom, 2016, pp. 71–72). Without getting too technical, the bottom line is that the peak speed of our biological neurons operates something like ten million times slower than the current microprocessor chip, and this is *only* the present stage of artificial *narrow* intelligence (ANI).

HOW FAR CAN IT GO?

As amazing as the advances in artificial *narrow* intelligence have been and will continue to be, it is even more extraordinary to realize that they will eventually pale in comparison to what will be forthcoming as we move toward the next stage of AI development, to that of artificial *general* intelligence and consistent human-level learning from machines. In many ways, this transition will reflect an increasing "inside job," from AI being primarily dependent on computer programmers and engineers for direction to learning on its own. Borrowing from psychology, a parallel might be the familiar concept of "locus of control," a useful framework for determining if a client in counseling or psychotherapy is more externally or internally directed and motivated. It is considered a major step forward in the client's growth and development when her locus of motivation shifts from looking outside of herself for direction to being guided more by her own internal "compass." Similarly, what will represent a major evolutionary leap forward for AI will be a shift away from an external to an internal locus of control, from exclusively needing computer programmers and engineers to "learn" to becoming more self-directed with its own learning. And, it is *already happening*, by way of the deep neural networks and the deep learning methods that we discussed earlier. Cognitive artificial intelligence, in other words, is already beginning to learn and therefore "evolve" on its own, through what is known as the process of recursive self-improvement and the transition from supervised to unsupervised learning. The victory of AlphaGo, a version of Google's DeepMind system, over the reining human Go champion, demonstrated that "Google's algorithm was able to use information provided to it by humans, and to learn on its own by playing against itself" (Hendler & Mulvehill, 2016, p. 70). Above all, writes Bostrom (2016), "the rising wave of technology improvements will pour increasing volumes of computational power into the turbines of the thinking machines" (pp. 88–89). The result will be a commensurate rise in the rate of computational speed, "initially because humans try harder to improve a machine intelligence that is showing spectacular promise, later because the machine intelligence itself becomes capable of driving further progress at digital speeds" (Bostrom, 2016, p. 94).

How did it happen so quickly, from a limited initial breakthrough in computer science to fast becoming a world-shattering and life-transforming phenomenon? How did computer-based technology, in a short span of fifty years, suddenly become the primary organizing force in the evolutionary process? In order to answer these questions in an informed and knowledge-able way, it is important to know something about Moore's law, which posits that "the number of transistors that can be fabricated on a single (computer) chip doubles every eighteen months or so" (Shanahan, 2015, p. xviii). For example, the standard computer chip of recent years consists of 14nm tech-nology, or more specifically 14nm transistors, which in its own right reflects an astonishing breakthrough in computer science. It might help to know that a nanometer measures all of a billionth of a meter, so that with computer technology already operating on an atomic scale, it is possible to assemble several billion high-speed transistors on a single chip. But, in keeping with Moore's law, this is about to give way to the manufacture of microprocessor chips with transistors half the size, "just 7 nanometers wide, or about 1/10,000th the width of a human hair" (Bigdoli, 2017, p. 28). And, there are reports of a 5nm chip and a 3nm to follow in years to come, even a 1nm that is on the drawing board, which begs the question, how atomic or even sub-atomic can the technology continue to go? We appear on the verge of an exponential growth of computer power, once again in keeping with Moore's law:

> First stated in 1965 by Gordon Moore, one of the founders of the Intel Corpo-ration, this simple law has helped revolutionize the world economy, generated fabulous new wealth, and irreversibly altered our way of life. When we plot the plunging price of computer chips and their rapid advancements in speed, processing power, and memory, you find a remarkably straight line going back fifty years. . . .Exponential growth is often hard to grasp, since our minds think linearly. It is so gradual that you sometimes cannot experience the change at all. But over decades, it can completely alter everything around us. (Kaku, 2011, pp. 22–23)

But, how far can researchers go with the present technology, with the ever-shrinking computer chip, before they hit the proverbial wall dictated by the universal laws of physics? There are indications already that Moore's law is coming to an end, when classical computer technology cannot continue to reduce the size of transistors in half as quickly, in every eighteen months or so. "At some point, it will be physically impossible to etch transistors in this way that are the size of atoms" (Kaku, 2011, p. 46). True, the technology is still astounding, with reports that 5nm and 3nm chips will at some point follow the 7nm, and that if researchers continue to develop a 1nm chip it could take computational power and processing speed to a whole new level. Even so, the coming advances may not come as quickly and predictably as they have before, in the past fifty years, guided by Moore's law. "You can even calculate roughly when Moore's law will finally collapse: when you finally hit transistors the size of individual atoms" (Kaku, 2011, p. 46). And then what? Will computer technology, and with it the further development of machine learning, collapse as well, making the whole discussion of the technological singularity and artificial *general* intelligence, let alone artificial *super*intelligence, moot? Even if Moore's law is coming to an end, I would urge caution in drawing the conclusion that the deceleration of technological growth and change is inevitable, as if there is necessarily a one-to-one correspondence.

Whatever the future longevity of Moore's law, the futurist Ray Kurzweil (2004) has argued that "there are more than enough new computing technologies now being researched, including three-dimensional silicon chips, optical computing, crystalline computing, DNA computing, and quantum computing, to keep the law of accelerating returns as applied to computation going for a long time" (p. 390). Indeed, given the research and recent breakthroughs emerging from the latter, the world of quantum computing, we can already begin to see that in the not-too-distant future, quantum computers will, in the words of Israeli researcher Dorit Aharonov (2015), "provide an exponential speedup over classical computers" given the "extravagant computational power of quantum mechanics" (pp. 329–330). She adds, "A different way to say this is that, as we believe today, the computational complexity exhibited by many-body quantum systems is exponentially more powerful than that of classical systems" (Aharonov, 2015, p. 330). Work on the quantum computer may go beyond the parameters of Moore's law, in other words will take a while longer to perfect than some eighteen months, but when it is eventually introduced in coming years, the rate of accelerating returns with computational power and processing speed will advance even more dramatically. But that is not all that is in the works. There is also, as Kurzweil (2004) notes, the emergence of optical computing, which "aims to drastically accelerate artificial-intelligence computations—to light speed" (Matteson, 2017). Just to be clear, this will not be computing at *seeming* light speed, but rather quite literally at the speed of light by way of photons, tiny particles of light. Without having to rely on the slower, not to mention less energy-efficient, electronics-based computer chip, the new optical chip architecture "could in principle speed up artificial-intelligence computations by orders of magnitude" (Matteson, 2017).

Faster computers, whether they are in the present classical and/or the future quantum or optical realm, "make it easier to create machine intelligence" (Bostrom, 2016, p. 295), and therefore increase the likelihood that artificial *general* or human-level intelligence will occur. On the one hand, accelerating progress in computer hardware and the semiconductor industry increases the likelihood of a faster "takeoff" for machine intelligence, yet on the other hand "it reduces the amount of time available for solving the control problem and for humanity to reach a more mature stage of civilization" (Bostrom, 2016, pp. 295–296). With artificial *narrow* intelligence (ANI) already well developed and clearly upon us, it is quite possible that human-level machine intelligence will not be far behind. This presupposes immediate thoughtful reflection about the potential ramifications, good *and* bad, for the human individual and for human civilization, while there is still time *before* the takeoff occurs. For example, we can already see in this increasing age of digitization and automation, in the ANI stage, that for all the beneficial advances of artificial intelligence, for the way it can improve and simplify my life and yours, it still poses an existential risk for humanity. In the New York area, we have now moved to what is known as "cashless tolling" on bridges and highways, which is another way of saying that notwithstanding the convenience of not having to stop and pay toll, there are fewer and fewer employed *human* toll collectors. Similarly, more and more of us prefer the automated self-checkout at the supermarket, for convenience and for timesaving, without always being mindful of the impact on the *human* workforce. When it comes to personal banking, we simply use the ATM machine to withdraw and even now deposit money, all without any help from a *human* teller. And, the steady decline of manufacturing employment in the American heartland, due to automation, reveals that we have already passed a pivotal point of no return, that "bringing back" these manufacturing jobs, the rallying cry of certain politicians, is at best an illusion or even worse a cynical political ploy. At the very least, it reflects a profound ignorance of the current situation, an inability and/or unwillingness to see the forest for the trees, for all the while we get sidetracked in the easy rhetoric of bringing back the familiar ways of the past, cognitive AI continues to evolve faster and faster.

Keeping in mind the challenges of living in a digital age, that with the continuing evolution of AI comes an existential risk, Bostrom (2016) notes that "the potential downside for human workers is therefore extreme," for if we see "a sufficient reduction in the demand for human labor, wages would fall below the human subsistence level" (p. 197). This has prompted considerable debate among economists, focused on the issue, pro and con, of a universal basic income (UBI) in the face of growing technological unemployment. At the moment, how far we get with the discussion of UBI is anyone's guess, for it will require not only input from economists, but also from those working in the halls of government, politicians and policymakers and ultimately lawmakers with the power to legislate. But this may be little more than wishful thinking, given the toxicity of our present political climate. More than a few of our leaders have become preoccupied with things that divide rather than unite us, with what Freud (1961) would have called the "narcissism of minor differences" (p. 68), leading to a stupefying inability to get much done of any consequence. At a time when we are on the verge of momentous change, when we can even see it unfolding right before us on a daily basis, we hear little if anything from our leaders that could be construed as a *genuinely* hopeful vision of the future. "Precisely because technology is now moving so fast, and parliaments and dictators alike are overwhelmed by data they cannot process quickly enough, present-day politicians are thinking on a far smaller scale than their predecessors a century ago" (Harari, 2017, p. 381).

It may or may not help to know that this is not entirely the fault of those in power, for no one, including politicians, economists, religious leaders, even the computer scientists and engineers themselves, can fully understand let alone predict what will be the eventual outcome of the technology revolution, both short- and long-term. Take the Google search algorithm, for example: while it is developed by huge teams of experts, "each member understands just one part of the puzzle, and nobody really understands the algorithm as a whole" (Harari, 2017, p. 398). Thus, if the computer programmers themselves cannot fully understand algorithmic technology as a whole, and where the advances in machine learning will soon take us, then perhaps in fairness to our government leaders, we are expecting too much. As machine intelligence continues to evolve at an accelerated rate, "policies, standards, and some form of governance will need to be established (and regularly updated) to maintain human and machine integrity," but, and herein is the dilemma, "developing these standards will require skills that few people possess today" (Hendler & Mulvehill, 2016, p. 167). For now, nobody in the American government has any idea what to do with the pressing issues of technology and artificial intelligence, nor can anyone even remotely predict where the country will be twenty years from now. "Besides, by the time the cumbersome government bureaucracy makes up its mind about cyber regulation, the Internet will have morphed ten times" (Harari, 2017, pp. 379).

It is something of a catch-22 situation, for while there is considerable confusion about and/or avoidance of the present technological revolution, the pressing and urgent issues we are facing require immediate attention, reflection, and action. We have already noted the potential for greater technological unemployment, as artificial intelligence becomes more and more integrated into human society, integrates itself further into our social fabric. For example, research is underway and fairly well along in the pursuit of automated self-driving cars and trucks, which has the potential for making the roads safer while at the same time eliminating the need for *human* taxi, Uber, and truck drivers. In terms of the latter, it would be "the first time that machines take direct aim at an entire class of blue-collar work in America," putting at risk "one of the most common jobs in many states, and one of the last remaining careers that offer middle-class pay to those without a college degree" (Kitroeff, 2016). The emerging trend of greater workplace automation, with profound implications for a workforce already beleaguered, has prompted Harari (2017) to conclude that "in the twenty-first century we might witness the creation of a massive new unworking class," with people who will not merely be unemployed but also *unemployable* (p. 330). What might the implications be for pastoral, spiritual, and clinical practitioners, whose study and training in developmental theory and perhaps even in career counseling was premised to a certain extent on the pre-automation world of the "social contract," where it is assumed that future employment in some gainful shape or form awaits any diligent graduate of high school or college? This is most certainly not the world we live in anymore, nor is it the world our clients and congregants live in either. And, how do we as educators go about helping students prepare for the future, when in truth no one knows what the world and the job market will look like ten years from now, let alone twenty or thirty? Harari (2017) makes clear that in spite of the familiar and highfalutin political rhetoric, "the crucial problem is not creating new jobs," but rather "creating new jobs that humans perform better than algo-rithms." He adds, with something of a warning:

> Since we do not know how the job market would look in 2030 or 2040, already today we have no idea what to teach our kids. Most of what they currently learn at school will probably be irrelevant by the time they are forty. Tradition-ally, life has been divided into two main parts: a period of learning followed by a period of working. Very soon this traditional model will become utterly obsolete, and the only way for humans to stay in the game will be to keep learning throughout their lives, and to reinvent themselves repeatedly. (p. 331)

INTELLIGENCE DECOUPLING FROM CONSCIOUSNESS

With machine intelligence fast gaining on biological intelligence, it is under-standable that we are beginning to see more focused discussion of the digital technologies ever before us, and how they have already altered the trajectory of human development and evolution. Lest we assume that these technologi-cal developments are, in the words of Susan Greenfield (2015), "an extreme and far-fetched scenario," something of "a sci-fi fantasy on par with time travel," we need to be very clear that *they are all starting to happen right now*" (p. 259). Human beings have already adapted in large measure to life on the screen, and will continue to do so to a far greater extent with future generations, as technology becomes the very "air" that we breathe. How could it not be, when babies today are spending considerable time in what is known, commercially, as an "Apptivity Seat?" This is a product introduced a few years ago by Fischer-Price, "a potty-training seat complete with an iPad holder, presumably to complement an infant lifestyle where the recliner in which the baby may spend many hours is also dominated by a screen" (Greenfield, 2015, p. 8). But digital technologies are not simply changing *what we do* as human beings; they are in fact rapidly changing *who we are* as a species, our very human nature, which will be the focus of subsequent chapters.

We would do well to immediately put this on the front-burner of our theological reflection and discourse, even if the scientific researchers are unable to precisely pinpoint a future date for the arrival of more advanced forms of machine intelligence. Murray Shanahan (2015) helps us to see that trying to pin down a precise date(s) is little more than a distraction, for "it is enough that there is a significant probability of the arrival of artificial super-intelligence at some point in the twenty-first century for its potentially enormous impact on humanity to command our attention today" (p. 162). Note the choice of words coming from a respected authority on the subject: there is a *significant probability* of the arrival of artificial *super*intelligence at some point in the twenty-first century, which presupposes that artificial *general* intelligence or human-level machine intelligence ushered in by the technological singularity will have already taken place. "It does not matter," argues Shanahan (2015), "what the timetable is, unless you are hoping for the singularity to occur just in time to catalyze medical research that will prolong your life" (p. 163). He adds, perhaps with Apptivity-Seat babies of the present in mind: "But more important than your life or mine is the world we bequeath to future generations, and this is likely to be profoundly reshaped by the advent of human-level AI" (p. 163). In fairness, not all computer researchers share the "probability view" that we are approaching an intelligence explosion. Jaron Lanier (2017), for example, in his recent book, *Dawn of the New Everything*, has written that "my position is that in a given year, no matter how far we project into the future, the best possible [virtual reality] system will never achieve complete coverage of all the human senses or measurement of everything there is to be measured from a person" (p. 49). To which we might want to ask, so what if it does not fully achieve the level of or "complete coverage" of human consciousness? Do we then move on from the issue, tabling it for another time much further into the future, if at all? "Whatever [virtual reality] is," Lanier continues (2017), "it is always chasing toward an ultimate destination that probably cannot ever be reached," although by his own admission, a profound understatement to be sure, "not everyone agrees with me about that" (p. 49).

I would argue that it is a combination of things that have been keeping us from taking up the issue more in earnest and with a greater sense of urgency, from moving it to the forefront of our theological reflection, not the least of which is a lack of perfect agreement within the scientific community. Added to this is the fact that pastoral and spiritual practitioners are so often steeped in *critical* theological reflection and a hermeneutics of suspicion, which I myself wholeheartedly embrace, even while recognizing that there are times when we take our critical thinking so far on this or that detail that we can miss the bigger picture, the proverbial forest for the trees. Even without a precise future date, there is already enough evidence to give us pause and carefully reflect on the possibility, the *probability* even that human-level machine intelligence could very well be developed in a matter of decades, and perhaps with it *super*intelligence. We do well *not* to wait to "cross that bridge" when we get to it, whether it be decades from now or longer, for by then the window for deep and meaningful reflection will have passed, hastened by the accelerated pace of machine learning. If we think that even now, in the present stage of artificial *narrow* intelligence, we have great difficulty keeping up with the proliferation of technology, that human beings are already in the words of Robert Kegan (1998), "in over our heads," we can only imagine what the feeling will be like when artificial *general* or human-level intelligence is upon us. "Sapiens," writes Hararai (2017), "evolved in the African savannah tens of thousands of years ago, and [our] algorithms are just not built to handle twenty-first century data flows" (p. 393). The moment for in-depth and sustained theological reflection, the moment to cultivate and strengthen our unique human attributes such as attentional control and mindful awareness, is before us, as is the moment to determine how life can still be lived as much as possible on our own terms, on *human* terms. If we instead adopt a wait-and-see attitude, the moment will surely come and go, in less time than we may think, for the digital technologies will not be marking time with us. Rather, technology will continue to advance and evolve at seeming and perhaps eventually at literal light speed, making the challenge for us to keep up with it all and to slow down for a quiet contemplative moment of reflection that much greater.

The other issue for us not to get hung up with is the matter of consciousness, specifically if and when artificial intelligence will gain self-awareness and self-understanding of its own mental processes, developing subjective experience as it were. This is another distraction that can reinforce a wait-and-see attitude, further postponing in-depth theological reflection of a most pressing issue. We can thank Hollywood for much of the misinformation, how it depicts in film and television that artificial intelligence, whether it be the Terminator or some other sinister robotic form, only becomes a matter of urgent concern when it reaches the level of consciousness. "Science fiction movies generally assume that in order to match and surpass human intelligence, computers will have to develop consciousness" (Harari, 2017, p. 314). But will they? It is of course entirely possible that machine intelligence will one day cross the threshold of consciousness, but in all likelihood this is on the more distant future horizon, as it is not the immediate focus of much of the current scientific research. Rather, as the term suggests, it is developing a human-level artificial *intelligence* that drives today's research, which is not at all synonymous with artificial *consciousness*. This is where someone as brilliant and knowledgeable as Lanier (2017) seems to get sidetracked, focused more on the future of artificial consciousness than on artificial superintelligence. In a relatively short span of time, computer-based intelligence has advanced exponentially, and will continue to do so in coming years, but as

Lanier indicates, computers are not on the verge of becoming conscious anytime soon. As far as we know, writes Harari (2017), the computers of today "are no more conscious than their prototypes in the 1950s," so that while there has been nothing less than a stunning advance in computer intelligence, "there has been exactly zero advance in computer consciousness" (pp. 313–314). Perhaps Lanier's comments, then, could prompt us to table the issue, maybe revisiting it again for reflection and discussion at an indefinite time in the future, seeing that computer consciousness is not any further along than it was in the beginning of computer science. This would be a serious mistake, for what we are still witnessing firsthand and living through is a momentous revolution of another kind: "intelligence is decoupling from consciousness" (Harari, 2017, p. 314).

Historically the two have always evolved together, a higher-order form of intelligence side by side with consciousness, coalescing into a conscious intelligence characteristic of human beings. For example, when it came to tasks requiring a higher-order intelligence, whether in the context of agriculture, manufacturing, transportation, and/or medicine, it was *conscious* human beings alone that could perform them. But, as we are learning, the landscape has been changing dramatically with the development of powerful digital technologies and new types of non-conscious intelligence, which can greatly exceed human performance. After all, "these tasks are based on pattern recognition, and non-conscious algorithms may soon excel human consciousness in recognizing patterns" (Harari, 2017, p. 314). Ultimately, the route that leads to the emergence of artificial *general* or human-level intelligence and beyond, i.e., *super*intelligence, may not go by way of consciousness at all, the laborious route taken by biological and organic evolution over the course of eons. "The evolution of inorganic computers may completely bypass these narrow straits, charting a different and much quicker course to superintelligence" (Harari, 2017, p. 314). As computer-based intelligence decouples from consciousness, the issue of whether AI is self-aware and can therefore feel and understand becomes less relevant (Kaku, 2014, pp. 239–240). At least for now, it is a distraction from more pressing issues that need our immediate theological reflection, such as the eventual merger of conscious (human) intelligence with a more powerful and algorithmically precise non-conscious (artificial) intelligence. For Harari (2017), it raises a novel question:

> Which of the two is really important, intelligence or consciousness? As long as they went hand in hand, debating their relative value was an amusing pastime for philosophers. But in the twenty-first century this is becoming an urgent political and economic issue. And it is sobering to realize that, at least for armies and corporations, the answer is straightforward: intelligence is mandatory but consciousness is optional. (p. 314)

Whether computers cross the consciousness threshold or not is therefore of less immediate concern than the forthcoming intelligence explosion, something we are already seeing with the proliferation of artificial *narrow* intelligence (ANI), and will continue to see even more strikingly as machines approach human-level (*general*) intelligence (AGI). This reflects the ultimate learning potential of machines, which is vastly superior to that of biological intelligence, as well as the immense power and processing differential between AI and human beings. Put another way, with computer hardware rapidly improving, "the ultimate limits of hardware performance are vastly higher than those of biological substrates" (Bostrom, 2016, p. 73). The human brain's capacity to store and process information is indeed, in and of itself, rather remarkable, and yet when even compared to that of present-day ANI, let alone with that of human-level AGI in the future, there is really no comparison. As we discussed earlier, "one can get some magnitude of the gap by considering the speed differential between electronic components and nerve cells: even today's transistors operate on a timescale ten million times shorter than that of biological neurons" (Bostrom, 2016, p. 53). Biological neurons, then, are in a word, slow, when compared to the processing speed of computer intelligence, only emitting a nerve impulse or "spike" every few milliseconds. At first glance this sounds impressive, and in a way it certainly is, until we discover that "in the time it takes for a typical neuron to emit two spikes, a desktop computer running at a modest 3 GHz can perform more than ten million operations" (Shanahan, 2015, p. 29). What it illustrates is that inorganic computers and machines are on the "fast track" in terms of their evolutionary trajectory, already taking a different route from organic or biological evolution by way of the rapid advancement of artificial *intelligence*, which at least for now continues to decouple from consciousness. We are clearly witnessing firsthand the beginning of a momentous if not epochal revolution that is changing everything, even life itself, which I am arguing necessitates immediate and in-depth theological reflection. After billions of years of wandering inside the realm of organic compounds, life is about to "break out into the vastness of the inorganic realm, and will take shapes that we cannot envision even in our wildest dreams" (Harari, 2017, p. 45). We can only begin to imagine where this will take us, for after all "our wildest dreams are still the product of organic chemistry" (Harari, 2017, p. 45).

This is not necessarily to suggest a dystopian future, for the rapid development and evolution of machine intelligence could actually enhance the quality of human life, *if* we continue to develop and apply it wisely. The continuing development and evolution of machine intelligence is therefore a double-edged sword, on the one hand posing an existential risk unlike anything humanity has ever seen before, while on the other hand becoming a potentially powerful ally in helping us deal with other existential risks, such as those of an environmental, military, and/or medical nature. In terms of medicine, it is well known that even the most voracious doctor can only keep up with so much of the medical information that is available online and in massive databases, related to her particular field of expertise as well to specific medical conditions that she is treating. Trying to keep up with the vast amount of medical information that is produced each year, whether in books, journal articles, conference papers, clinical cases, and so forth is an impossible task for a human doctor, even for the most renowned medical expert. Perhaps then it is no surprise that in 2015, "the National Academy of Medicine reported that most people will receive an incorrect or late diagnosis at least once in their lives, sometimes with serious consequences," and also "cited one estimate that twelve million people—about five percent of adults who seek outpatient care—are misdiagnosed annually" (Bernstein, 2017).

Medical practitioners, despite the quality of their study and training and even advanced expertise, are after all human beings, and therefore like all of us subject to cognition distortions, emotional fluctuation, and inflated ego. But this is about to change in the direction of increased diagnostic precision, as medicine looks more and more to an ally with infinitely more medical information at its disposal, not to mention the capacity to peruse and process it thoroughly at a far more advanced rate of speed, namely artificial intelligence. IBM's supercomputer, who most of us know as "Watson" from its stellar performance a few years ago on the game show, *Jeopardy*, has since moved on to more important and noble endeavors, for example in the realm of medical diagnosis and with cancer diagnosis and oncology treatments. There are even predictions that it is well on the way to becoming the best doctor and diagnostician in the world:

> Watson is already capable of storing far more medical information than doctors, and unlike humans, its decisions are all evidence-based and free of cognitive biases and overconfidence. It is also capable of understanding natural language, generating hypotheses, evaluating the strength of those hypotheses, and *learning—not just storing data, but finding meaning in it.* (Friedman, 2014)

Healthcare and medicine is one of the prime examples of the way machine intelligence is coming to the aid of human beings, doctor and patient alike, an ally already in the pursuit of more precise diagnoses, medical interventions, and effective treatment strategies. Along with treating cancer more effectively, AI-based healthcare has helped researchers and practitioners greatly enhance the quality of life for those experiencing hearing and vision impairment, mental-health issues, and memory loss associated with aging. The cochlear procedure, for example, of surgically implanting an electronic hearing device to the back of the skull has improved the lives of many people around the world, young and old, restoring a sense of sound perception. My own father underwent the surgery a few years ago, and to his own amazement could once again hear the calls of songbirds that he had not been able to hear for decades. There are mental-health apps that can be downloaded on any smartphone, to enhance the therapeutic treatment of an anxious or depressed client by way of psycho-educational feedback and techniques. And, "memory assistive technologies are currently being developed to support people with mild forms of dementia," helping them to keep track of the day and time and manage daily tasks and events, and reminding them "about when to eat, go to an appointment, talk to a loved one, etc." (Hendler & Mulvehill, 2016, p. 110). One of the most remarkable of these assistive technologies is the implantable brain pacemaker, currently being developed to augment cognitive and memory function with patients diagnosed with Alzheimer's or Parkinson's disease (Hendler & Mulvehill, 2016, p. 111). As we confront a future with an aging population, a looming crisis as it were in the long-term healthcare of older adults, AI-based assistive technologies will be needed to have a realistic hope of meeting the growing demand for elder care. To bring this into sharper focus, it is estimated that "by 2050, the number of people age 65 and older with Alzheimer's disease may nearly triple, from 5.1 million to a projected 13.8 million, barring the development of medical breakthroughs to prevent or cure the disease" (Hendler & Mulvehill, 2016, p. 70).

Any breakthroughs in medicine from this point on will of course be AI-assisted, *must* be AI-assisted if we as a society hope to meet the healthcare demands of the present and future. At the same time, we cannot forget the inherent and striking double-edgedness of machine intelligence, for while it is a potentially powerful ally in enhancing the quality of human life, if used wisely, it also has the potential of fast becoming an existential risk to the future of humanity. Diverse theological narratives are starting to emerge in response to this momentous and pivotal moment in human history, to life in a digital age, some of which we could describe as narratives of hope while describing others as narratives of apprehension, if not fear. It is therefore to theological narratives, reflecting on the rise of digital technologies and machine intelligence, that we now turn our attention.

Chapter Two

Theological Narratives of Hope and Apprehension

Theological reflection on the momentous changes unfolding before us is already available, and therefore will serve as a useful guide for helping practitioners develop at least a neutral if not somewhat hopeful framework for viewing human life in a digital age. As I noted in the introduction, I find the correlational method put forward by Paul Tillich (1973) to be a useful starting point for holding theological perspectives and current scientific research in dialectical and dialogical tension. In a way it is reminiscent of the Swiss theologian Karl Barth's approach, "constructing theology with the Bible in one hand and the newspaper in the other" (Rosner, 2015, p. 52), a fundamental awareness that for theological discourse to be of value for lived human experience in the present day and age, it must have an informed understanding of the current socio-cultural landscape and of the emerging forces that are now central to the evolutionary process. This assumes that theology and religion will at the very least be in *dialogue* with science and technology, which in and of itself can be a productive conversation, although I would argue that as we move into an era of unprecedented change, dialogue will not be enough. More inclusive paradigms that help us better *integrate* current scientific research into our theological frameworks will be needed, as we attempt to navigate, for ourselves and for those in our care, the increasingly unique and unfamiliar terrain. I would also encourage *not* reverting to the familiar refrain of "there is nothing new under the sun," noting that human beings have been here countless times before, confronted by the changing times again and again down through the centuries, and will get through this transition like we have all the others. True, change has been a fundamental constant of human life from time immemorial, only now with the revolutionary advances in computational power and processing, combined with the unparalleled evolutionary speed of machine intelligence, the stakes have become infinitely higher. When we are talking about the approaching and inevitable unemployablity of large groups of human beings due to the algorithmic sophistication of AI, the decoupling of intelligence from consciousness with tasks requiring higher-order thinking, and the evolutionary transition from Homo to Techno sapiens, let us be clear, there *is* something new under the sun and it is changing the landscape *and* us irreversibly.

A COMPLEX COCKTAIL OF OPPORTUNITY AND THREAT

It may seem, intuitively, that the first order of business with our theological reflection is to try and figure out a way to deal with the advancing force of the digital technologies, to meaningfully engage the external "other," in this case technology, while simultaneously maintaining a certain level of distance. With Barbour's (1997) model in mind, this would constitute a dialogical form of relating to science: religion and theology are quite interested in current scientific research, particularly having to do with breakthroughs in computer intelligence, but when it is all said and done, when the stimulating and even meaningful dialogue with science is over, we return to our familiar theological framework. In so doing, we have managed to deal with technology, more or less, by reflecting on it theologically, and can now move on to other issues. While there is of course no shortage of other pressing issues that we must deal with, which also stand in need of our immediate theological reflection, we must be very clear that the advance and proliferation of technology is not simply one issue among many others. In seemingly no time at all, in a matter of a few decades, we have evolved into technologically dependent human beings, and we can only imagine what our technological dependence will be in the future. To assume that we need only *deal with* the science of technology, to merely approach it dialogically as an external issue and force, is fundamentally to miss the bigger picture that is unfolding right in front of us. As Ilia Delio (2008) has already noted, it cannot merely be a religious or theological way of dealing with technology, as if it were something completely external to who we are as human individuals and as a human species. With technology rapidly merging with our own human biology, and quite possibly in coming years forming a so-called singularity, we will need to develop new theological paradigms, sooner rather than later, which are much more inclusive and *integrative* of the current scientific research. Yet, even this might not go far enough, as technology continues to gain the upper hand as the major organizing force, not only of contemporary life but also of the evolutionary process, superseding biology in terms of primacy. "It is not enough," writes Delio (2008), "simply to come to terms with the integration of technology in daily life," but rather "we must begin to see technology as integral to the whole evolutionary process because it has driven us to a whole new level of culture and consciousness" (p. 163).

What this presupposes is the development of a thoroughgoing theology of technology, with the capacity to guide and sustain our in-depth reflection of human life in a digital world. As I noted earlier, I find the work of Karl Rahner (1978) helpful in this regard, in particular his theology of *Vorgriff*, a pre-apprehension of infinite mystery and infinite reality, a "pure openness for absolutely everything, for being as such" (p. 20). Rahner, in embracing the fundamental dynamism of human life and of all creation, has put forward a theological anthropology that has a distinct future orientation to it, combined with an evolutionary understanding of human beings. "*Vorgriff*, as discerned from humanity's own transcendental inquiry, can serve as a framework drawn from human experience to *analogously* identify similar instantiations of self-presence that is the divine nature of God" (Fisher, 2015, p. 35). God's loving and caring presence in the world is certainly manifested in human beings who are created *imago Dei*, but with all that we are learning in recent years by way of the natural sciences, astrophysics, and quantum mechanics, it is quite clear that divine energy and creativity is also manifested elsewhere, in fact throughout the entire world and cosmos. "We now know too much about the dynamics of the natural world to maintain the anthropocentric claim that it is only humans who are 'favored' by God" (Fisher, 2015, p. 35–36). More immediately, what about our increasing knowledge of the digital world, our current understanding of what is presently before us, namely artificial narrow intelligence, as well as a pre-apprehension of what will likely follow it in the future: human-level machine intelligence and ultimately superintelligence? Could this be another manifestation of God's divine presence and creativity, or is it something completely unrelated? Epistemologically, how do we even *know*, and can we ever be entirely sure? On the threshold of unprecedented change, "we now stand in the intellectual space where sharing an 'I-thou' relationship with another species, a computer program, or an uploaded friend is an imagined possibility" (Fisher, 2015, p. 36).

To state the obvious, we have entered uncharted territory, so that in developing a theology of technology, it will be important to do so with a spirit of openness and humility. Science has taught us a great deal down through the centuries, even more in recent years, such as the staggering vastness of cosmic space and at the other end the equally stunning region of subatomic space, reminding us of the grandeur of the universe and God's creation, while also revealing just how little we know about it. We would do well to keep this in mind as we move forward developing a theology of technology, as we reflect on the immense learning potential of machines that are vastly superior to our own biological intelligence, and as we carefully ponder God's presence and role in the evolution of intelligent machines. We cannot afford to put this off until later, for already the future is bearing down on us and on those in our pastoral, spiritual, and/or clinical care. Ronald Cole-Turner (2000) asks, rhetorically:

> Can theology—that communal process by which the church's faith seeks to understand—can theology aim at understanding technology? Can we put the words *God* and *technology* together in any kind of meaningful sentence? Can theology guess what God is doing in today's technology? Or by our silence do we leave it utterly godless? Can we have a theology of technology that comprehends, gives meaning to, dares to influence the direction and sets limits to this explosion of new powers? (p. 101)

If the answer is at best a tepid "yes" to putting *God* and *theology* together in our theological reflection, or at worst a defiant "no," in either case we put ourselves at risk given the rapid advance of digital technologies. How so? With technology already infiltrating the very fabric of human society to a degree of undisputable and life-sustaining dependence, our present and future development as human beings, both individual and collective, is now intertwined with and dependent on the powerful digital technologies with which we are merging. Whether we *like* this evolutionary turn of events or not, whether or not we believe it is the way life *should* be, is increasingly irrelevant, for as I have noted, we are already well beyond the point of no return. A theological stance of *acceptance*, rather than resistance or even mere resignation for that matter, is necessary if we hope to navigate the new terrain effectively. And, as we learn from acceptance- and mindfulness-based therapeutic approaches, such as Acceptance and Commitment Therapy (ACT) and Mindfulness-Based Cognitive Therapy (MBCT), acceptance is not synonymous with liking or wanting a particular situation. Instead, "acceptance is actively entering into the reality of what is rather than attaching to how we wish it to be or how much we like the way it is" (Roemer & Orsillo, 2009, p. 116). In this particular context, it is entering into the reality of digital technology and machine learning, in order to better grasp the landscape that we, and those in our care, must now navigate. To avoid the present reality, ostensibly in order to keep God and technology separate, or simply to treat the science of digital technology and artificial intelligence as merely one issue among many others, is to put our own future development as human beings at greater risk. "Without taking modern science seriously as revelatory of a living God, and evolution as the way God delights in creating anew, we are aiming to devolve" (Delio, 2013, p. 202). If there was ever a time to hold the Bible in one hand and a newspaper in the other, or more specifically to "hold the scriptures in one hand and *Scientific American* in the other" (Delio, 2013, p. 202), that time is now. On some level, God is actively involved in the present evolutionary transition that is merging technology, biology, and society, for "divine love evolves the universe as it leans into an unknown future" (Delio, 2013, p. 202).

This reflects a theology of *Vorgriff*, the pre-apprehension of divine and infinite reality that is dynamically and perpetually moving us and the world and the whole universe into the mystery of the future, an openness for absolutely everything, to use Rahner's words, in keeping with the Ignatian method of finding God in all things. This is not, to be sure, merely an exercise in esoteric speculation, as if theology in the abstract can ever be an end in and of itself, without having any meaningful connection with the present-day lived experience of human beings. Rather, in building on Rahner's (1978) theology of *Vorgriff*, I am encouraging the development of a pastoral and practical theology that purposely intersects with the hopes and fears of people living in a digital age, in particular those who are and will be most at risk with the inevitable advancement of AI. As machine learning continues to evolve, exponentially increasing its algorithmic power and speed, certain groups of people will be most vulnerable, such as those possessing labor skills that are less suited for a digital age or simply that are no longer any match for machine intelligence. Developing an in-depth theology of technology, and of the coming merger of humans and machines, has therefore become a more necessary and urgent matter, while there is still a window of opportunity. This assumes that we can resist the temptation to revert to a wait-and-see attitude, marking time until machines reach human-level intelligence. By then, the window of opportunity for developing a meaningful theology of technology will be closing, and we will have no choice but to do our reflection, so to speak, on the run. Harari (2017) uses the metaphor of a train pulling out of the station, even going so far as to say that it could very well be the final train to leave the station known as Homo sapiens proper:

> Those [of us] who miss the train will never get a second chance. In order to get a seat on it you need to understand twenty-first century technology, and in particular the powers of biotechnology and computer algorithms. These powers are far more potent than steam and the telegraph, and they will not be used merely for the production of food, textiles, vehicles, and weapons. The main products of the twenty-first century will be bodies, brains, and minds, and the gap between those who know how to engineer bodies and brains and those who do not will be far bigger than the gap between . . . Sapiens and Neanderthals. (p. 275)

For now, we still have a window of time and opportunity to reflect very intentionally on the present moment, in order to develop a theology of technology that resonates deeply with people living in a digital age, a theology that has the capacity to hold together, dialectically, our narratives of hope and fear. It will necessarily need to be a theology of the so-called middle way, between hopefulness and apprehension, between technology viewed exclusively as opportunity or as threat. It is both of these, and whether it ultimately becomes more of an opportunity or more of a threat has to do with the way we continue to develop, handle, and apply the powerful medium of digital technologies, which interestingly and perhaps paradoxically makes it more of a *human* issue or problem. I will have more to say about this later. In the present digital age, we are being offered, writes Susan Greenfield (2015), "an unprecedented and complex cocktail of opportunity and threat," so that "it would be simplistic in the extreme to think of the powerful and pervasive new digital lifestyle as either the apotheosis of human existence or the most toxic culture ever" (p. 23). To view the digital age exclusively and pejoratively as the latter, as little more than a toxic culture with diminishing meaning and value, is to risk alienating the "digital natives" among us, those young adults and younger who have no direct experience of the supposed simpler time before the proliferation of technology. Indeed, the important distinction to keep in mind is that "digital natives know no other way of life other than the culture of Internet, laptop, and mobile" (Greenfield, 2015, p. 6). A fear-based theology that views the digital culture mostly as an "all-bad object," with barely any redeeming value if any, will have little or more likely no resonance with those who have known no other way of life.

This is not at all meant to suggest merely acquiescing to the advancement of digital technologies and machine intelligence, adopting a theological stance of resignation to the inevitable. There is, to be sure, plenty of justification for having some measure of healthy apprehension, for as we discussed in the previous chapter, artificial intelligence is very much a double-edged sword, simultaneously posing both an existential opportunity *and* risk. In terms of the risk, we need only recall the threat to human employment, with particular groups of laborers increasingly unemployable, and the threat to human consciousness, as intelligence continues its decoupling maneuver, charting a different and more expeditious route to superintelligence and thereby rendering consciousness optional. The advancement of machine intelligence and learning clearly poses an existential risk to our collective identity, to what has made us uniquely human for millennia, if not to our very survival as a human species. "This may sound like hyperbole, but today's emerging technologies have a potency never before seen" (Shanahan, 2015, p. xxi). With a window of time and opportunity still before us, it is important to develop a pastoral and practical theology that takes very seriously the existential risk posed by AI and the potential threat to what is uniquely human, aiming to preserve something of the uniqueness of human identity. Otherwise, there is potential for "so completely changing the way we see the world that we lose the richer, more embodied, more emotional and complicated meaning of our human relationships, our yearnings, our failures, and our attempts to begin anew" (Cole-Turner, 2011b, p. 201). The existential threat is therefore nothing short of a complete alteration of human consciousness.

BEHOLD, I AM DOING A NEW THING

Technology in general and artificial intelligence in particular is, as we have noted, something of a double-edged sword, for while it clearly poses an existential risk to humanity, it also offers us in other ways something of an existential opportunity. Technology, in other words, has the capacity not only to diminish but also to enhance our humanity, of course with an important caveat: *if* we can find ways to use the medium wisely, justly, and with great care. Thirty years ago, Ian Barbour (1992) had already grasped, perhaps with a bit of prescience, the double-edged nature of technology, arguing with conviction in *Ethics in an Age of Technology,* the publication of his Gifford Lectures, that the welfare of humankind requires and even needs "a creative technology that is economically productive, ecologically sound, socially just, and personally fulfilling" (p. 25). Additionally, the welfare of humankind needs, in a digital age characterized by the rapid advance of machine intelligence, a creative *theology* of technology, which can embrace the unprecedented change and existential opportunity before us even while trying, as Ted Peters (2007) has suggested, to help "guide that change towards wholesome and loving ends" (p. 182). In a way, this echoes Rahner's theology of *Vorgriff,* for helping to guide the unprecedented change toward wholesome and loving ends presupposes a pre-apprehension of the divine presence that is ever moving us and the world into the mystery of the future. "The image of God, then, is a constant call *forward*," so that "our true humanity is *eschatological*" (Lebacqz, 2011, p. 58). It is learning to find God in all things, in the existential opportunity of the present moment and in what is to come, guided by a pre-apprehension of the infinite and loving divine presence. A theology of technology can therefore offer urgent meaning for the present digital age, something that science, its astounding breakthroughs notwithstanding, cannot do. In fact, it remains the "one huge drawback" for science; that is, it has far less if anything to say about questions of value and meaning, even if "human societies cannot survive without such value judgments" (Harari, 2017, p. 238).

A theology of technology must necessarily fill this void, for even if we are heading into or perhaps already in the midst of an era of unprecedented change, hastened by the stunning breakthroughs in computer science, we still need to make sense of it all, for human beings are fundamentally meaning makers. If computer science stops short of addressing the fundamental value and meaning of its own technological breakthroughs, in keeping with the historical parameters of the scientific method, then theology must step in, and in particular *pastoral* and *practical* theology, to develop a framework that helps those in our care reflect on the meaning of lived human experience in a digital age. Our theological framework will have to be spacious enough to include and even welcome very diverse human attitudes and emotions, manifested in personal and collective narratives ranging from apprehension and fear to anticipation and hope. This again reflects a theology of the middle way, holding together in dialectical tension the existential risk *and* opportunity posed by the rapid advance and proliferation of digital technologies. Moreover, it is an affirmative response to the rhetorical questions put forward earlier by Cole-Turner (2000): theology can, it *must* aim at understanding and helping to clarify the existential value and meaning of technology, the new thing that God is doing in the present day and age, thus making it perfectly clear that it is indeed possible and necessary to put God and technology together in our theological reflection. Nor will it come a minute too soon, given that the evolutionary transition has already begun merging technology with biology and in turn with human society.

The evolutionary merger of humans and machines is already underway, even if we still have a ways to go before AI achieves consistent and comprehensive human-level learning, and before there is a more complete human-computer interface. How do we as spiritual and clinical practitioners make sense of this evolutionarily momentous turn of events, for ourselves and for our congregants and clients? For example, does the extraordinary growth and rapid advancement of digital technologies, in a matter of a few decades, reflect divine presence and creativity, God once again "doing a new thing" in the world if we put it in the language of the prophet (Isaiah 43:19)? Or, does the increasing power and proliferation of technology reflect the opposite, a more sinister development that has nothing to do with God and with divine presence, but rather with fallen human beings trying to "play God?" My own view is that it is *not* the latter, for this would mean, theologically, that for all intents God has suddenly gone absent from the evolutionary process of creation, nowhere to be found. Instead, the words of the prophet are a reminder that God is forever in the process of moving the creation forward, perpetually doing a new thing, in this instance by way of digital technologies and machine intelligence. This offers something that is theologically hopeful, not in the embrace of technology as an all-good object that we hope will somehow bring us utopia if not salvation, but rather in the prophetic words that God is *always* doing a new thing in the creative and evolutionary process, even in the present digital age with the emergence of technologically enhanced human beings. A pastoral and practical theology of technology allows for the creative development of digital technologies and, from a Christian standpoint, "realizes that human creativity and the emergence of techno sapiens give new expression to Christ in evolution" (Delio, 2008, p. 180). The incarnation reveals the divine intention to be radically immanent in the world, and for Christ to be in complete solidarity with human experience. "Because we humans are in evolution we must see Christ in evolution as well—Christ's humanity is our humanity, Christ's life is our life" (Delio, 2008, p. 180).

The existential threat to human experience and even human existence, posed by technology and machine intelligence, is quite real, but so is the existential opportunity, if human beings can find ways to help guide the evolutionary process toward loving and hopeful ends. In the previous chapter, we noted the positive impact that AI-based assistive technologies have already been making in the field of healthcare, and will continue to make even more powerfully in the coming years, greatly enhancing and improving the quality of life for many people of all ages. Examples include implant technology designed to improve and even in some cases restore hearing and vision, prosthetic devices featuring sophisticated artificial limbs, which have been a godsend for people throughout the world and particularly for military veterans and victims of war, and mental-health apps that enhance and support the work of counseling and psychotherapy and the ongoing treatment of psychological disorders. Overall, medical diagnosis and treatment has become increasingly more precise, thanks to an AI-based approach to healthcare and the development of AI-assistive technologies, reflecting the existential opportunity of machine intelligence guided toward loving and hopeful ends. And to think that this is only the beginning, as brain neurotechnology becomes further developed and perfected. Earlier we noted memory-assistive technologies, such as the implantable brain pacemaker, a neuroprosthetic device that augments cognitive and memory function in the treatment of Alzheimer's disease. As impressive and beneficial as a brain pacemaker can be, a far more advanced neuroprosthetic device is in the works, involving a neural structure of the brain no less, namely an artificial hippocampus:

> Professor Theodore Berger and his research team at the University of Southern California has made remarkable progress towards developing an artificial hippocampus, a structure of the brain which plays important roles in the consolidation of information from short-term memory to long-term memory and that also contributes to spatial navigation. Alzheimer's disease is known to damage the hippocampus and affects about 5.3 million people in the United States alone. Thus, creating an artificial hippocampus may help millions suffering from a serious and debilitating neurological disease; but . . . cyborg technologies designed to assist people based on medical necessity may also have the effect, intended or not, of contributing to our cyborg future and eventual merger with machines. (Barfield, 2015, p. 106)

There is certainly a trade-off, for technology as a double-edged sword offers, as we have been saying, an unprecedented and complex cocktail of both opportunity and threat. It appears we cannot have one without the other, so that as we guide technology in further enhancing the quality of human life

and well-being, we simultaneously contribute to our own merger with machines. Increasingly, more of this is beyond our control, as technology and
artificial intelligence takes on more of a life of its own, "evolving" on its own
as it were. It has now become the dominant organizing force in the evolutionary process, so central to human life that even if we could thwart any further
technological development, we would witness immediate economic collapse,
both nationally and globally. Moreover, attempting to keep humans separate
from machine intelligence, in other words exclusively addressing the existential threat without at the same time aiming to help guide technology toward
the loving end of enhancing human well-being, is much too one-sided. We
need only recall that "[AI technologies] help people solve big problems on a
personal level (me, my health, daily existence), at the community level
(crime, traffic), and those facing [humankind] (clean air, clean water, global
warming)" (Hendler & Mulvehill, 2016, p. 10). In terms of the existential
opportunity, for example with war veterans, we can add that AI-based medical research is also making advances in the treatment of brain injury and
post-traumatic memories, again by way of neurotechnology and neuropros-
thetics. It does however involve our increasing merger with machine intelligence, which again is the trade-off:

> Sometimes to know where technology is headed, one needs to follow the
> money; this is especially true for cyborg technology. On this point, the Euro-
> pean Union has committed to spend $1.3 billion to study how the brain func-
> tions, and in the United States, the Human Brain Project has received $1
> billion for basic research on brain science . . . both of these initiatives will
> provide critical information about the structure of neuronal circuits necessary
> to reverse engineer the brain (one way to create artificial general intelligence).
> Further, the combined $2.3 billion in funding for neuroscience research just
> mentioned, is not the complete funding picture. For example, in the United
> States the Defense Advanced Research Projects Agency (DARPA) has been
> one of the major government agencies funding research to develop brain chips
> and other technologies to interface the brain to computers. On this point,
> DARPA is currently working with different groups of researchers to develop a
> neuronal prosthetic implant that can be used to treat severe memory loss in
> human patients. The project is part of DARPA's Restoring Active Memory
> (RAM) program, aimed to help reinstate normal memory activity for the U.S.
> war veterans who have suffered some kind of brain injury. If successful, the
> program will be immensely beneficial for patients with schizophrenia, amne-
> sia, dementia, and other brain disorders. (Barfield, 2015, p. 105)

It would seem that in order to further enhance the quality of human life,
by way of computer intelligence and AI-assistive technologies, we will necessarily have to accept the fact of our inevitable merger with machines *and*
our evolutionary transition from Homo to Techno sapiens. We cannot, in
other words, have it both ways, continuing as individuals and as a society to

make greater use of digital technologies for our daily personal use, our healthcare needs, financial management, and so forth without coming to terms with the growing possibility of a technological singularity, when machines achieve artificial general (human-level) intelligence. To a large extent, it is already something of a moot issue, given the emergence of technology as the dominant organizing force within the evolutionary process. As we have been saying, the train, so to speak, left the station some time ago, so that we are already beyond the point of no return. But above and beyond the centrality of technology for the evolutionary process and for global economics, what about its importance for enhancing the quality of human life, the quality of "abundant life" if we use the language of Jesus (John 10:10)? To be sure, I would have a difficult time telling someone in my care, a client or a congregant, badly in need of a neuroprosthetic device to augment cognitive and memory function, that he or she should just leave well enough alone because the medical procedure borders on "playing God," that humans should know their place in the created order, that artificial intelligence after all poses an existential threat to human nature and existence. Not only would this be an obstacle to cultivating therapeutic rapport with the individual, my myopic tunnel vision would keep me from glimpsing the bigger picture, the very real possibility that God is using AI-assistive technologies toward wholesome and loving ends, toward the restoration of more abundant living.

The issue in urgent need of our reflection has to do with the inevitable evolutionary transition from Homo to Techno sapiens, given our reliance *and* dependence on computer technology and machine intelligence. We cannot have our personal digital assistants, GPS navigation, AI-based healthcare, and financial algorithms without it sooner or later reaching a tipping point, with our eventual and more complete merger with machines. Even now certain theological issues are beginning to emerge: if in fact we are in the midst of an evolutionary transition from Homo to Techno sapiens, then what are the implications for human nature, the focus of the next chapter? What constitutes human nature in a digital age of technological enhancement and modification? And, are technologically enhanced humans and eventually Techno sapiens still a reflection of the divine image, the *Imago Dei*? If our theology of technology leads us to conclude that the eventual arrival of Techno sapiens is yet another reflection of divine presence doing a new thing, the constant call forward into the future, then our human story and the story of creation and life on earth will need to make room for "another kind of being, a being with new and different capabilities" (Shanahan, 2015, p. 183). The possibility of a "new being" will be challenging for some of us to get our minds around, depending on the flexibility and/or rigidity of our theological framework. And yet, who of us can say that God cannot be doing a new thing in this way or that way, that God and technology are somehow mutually exclusive. It is reminiscent of where we have been before, historically, in keeping religion independent of science, separating theology from any discussion of evolution, and viewing humanity, "us," as the apotheosis of God's creation. To look at this through the lens of science can be instructive, for as Murray Shanahan (2015) observes, "it is surely the height of anthropocentric thinking to suppose that the story of the universe climaxes with human society and the myriad living brains embedded in it, marvelous as they are" (p. xxii). If we are to regard technology and artificial intelligence even partially as an existential opportunity, it "can only be grasped by stepping outside the human perspective altogether and adopting a more cosmological point of view" (Shanahan, 2015, p. xxii). Put more spiritually, it would be stepping outside of human hubris, getting out of our own way in order to more fully grasp and help lovingly guide the new thing that God is doing.

Reflecting on this from a more cosmological point of view has the potential of expanding our theological horizons as never before. It will not take too long to see that God has been doing a new thing again and again in creation and the universe for a very long time, *billions* of years in fact as we have been learning from astrophysicists, long before human beings ever walked the earth. Moreover, we are learning from biological engineering that here on earth "we are far from realizing the full potential of organic bodies," the implication being that "there is no reason to think that (Homo) sapiens is the last station" (Harari, 2017, p. 44). In fact, the next station could be right up ahead, with the arrival of Techno sapiens, and the merger of biology with technology. This is because bioengineering will not be taking a wait-and-see approach, waiting for biology and natural selection to take its good old time, as it has been doing for eons, until this species or that species emerges. Rather, bioengineers intend to take the human body and "rewrite its genetic code, rewire its brain circuits, alter its biochemical balance, and even grow entirely new limbs" (Harari, 2017, p. 44). This is a matter of extreme importance for theology, prompting us to reflect very intentionally on these and other questions of value and meaning, prompted by advances in human enhancement and modification. The coming merger of humans and machines, and with it the potential emergence of a new evolutionary species, namely Techno sapiens, invites us to revisit some of the most profound and deeply spiritual questions human beings can ask, only now as Shanahan (2015) has put it, they are thrown into an entirely new light:

> How should we live? How should we confront death? What does it mean to be human? What is mind? What is consciousness? What is our potential as a species? Do we have a purpose, and if so, what is it? What is our ultimate destiny? Whatever the future actually holds, looking at these questions through the lens of the singularity is enlightening. Philosophers ask these sorts of questions, and religions purport to answer them. (pp. 222–223)

With these timeless philosophical and religious questions in mind, he adds: "The hope is that artificial intelligence, far from destroying us, will help us realize our boldest aspirations while pursuing our highest ideals" (Shanahan, 2015, p. 226).

A FUNDAMENTAL *HUMAN* PROBLEM

The extent to which machine intelligence will ultimately be more opportunity than threat, or vice versa, interestingly has less to do with the technology itself and more to do with how we as human beings intend to utilize it going forward. Will we help guide the development of digital technologies toward just and loving ends, benefitting all people, no exceptions, even the "least" of these in the words of Jesus (Matthew 25:31–46), or will technology be used more in the service of power, greed, and profit, becoming a formidable dividing wedge that further extends and could even make permanent the gap between the haves and have-nots? It is therefore at bottom more of a *human problem* than anything, as it so often has been down through recorded history, whether we will put the raw material at our disposal, in this case technology, to good and loving use or not. Technology, in and of itself and like any other "raw material," is not good or bad, but rather a neutral entity; it simply "mirrors" the very best and the very worst of humanity. For example, in terms of putting social media and networking to good use, "the potential to spread information at breakneck speed in countries where information may be repressed or controlled is a vital tool," as is raising consciousness about urgent humanitarian and refugee crises, making use of crowdfunding to support disaster relief, and helping those in need of medical implants locate the most advanced treatment facilities (Greenfield, 2015, pp. 148–149). Conversely, by way of the same social media and networking, "some of the very worst aspects of being all too human . . . are now being given free rein throughout the uncharted territory of cyberspace" (Greenfield, 2015, p. 268), such as the untold cruelty of cyberbullying, the discord incited by Internet trolling, the online "grooming" of children and youth by sexual predators, and the hatching and development of terrorist plots.

It is not too difficult to see that there is a double-edgedness with social media, like technology in general, which to be clear is not because technology possesses this inherently, but rather has to do with how and in what ways human beings put it to use. Put another way, the existential opportunity and threat before us, two sides of the same coin as it were, has more to do with human beings and our own sense of human judgment than it does with the ethically and morally neutral digital technologies. Delio (2013), in *The Unbearable Wholeness of Being*, takes this a step further, going beyond "technology as neutral" to reframe it as a "good" in and of itself, in light of its central and primary importance in the evolutionary process and therefore in the created order. In understanding technology as a good, or perhaps simply as neutral if "good" is too much of a stretch for some of us, we can see that "in itself it is not the problem," for the more fundamental issue "is what we do with our technologies, what we expect of them, and how we relate to them that are problematic" (Delio, 2013, p. 204). To return to social media and networking, it is clear that most of the problems associated with it are not technological in nature, but rather have more to do with what *we* expect of it and how *we* relate to it. On the one hand, it is now far easier to keep up with friends and loved ones and colleagues, thanks to the global reach of this particular digital technology, so that we do not miss out on important developments in their lives. Nor do we miss out on important "breaking news" either, all the up-to-the-minute details about politics, world and national events, business and finance, sports, fashion, and so forth. The flip side, however, is that many of us have a pervasive anxiety that inevitably we are missing out on something, and/or we are not keeping up with others we respect and admire. If we look at this historically, we could say that "modern humanity is sick with FOMO—Fear of Missing Out—and though we have more choice than ever before, we have lost the ability to really pay attention to whatever we choose" (Harari, 2017, p. 366). I will be discussing the issue of attentional control and stability in greater detail in a later chapter.

Even when we do stop and pay attention to an alert or update from one of our many virtual communities or networks, sometimes it is not always in the best interests of our health and well-being. In my own counseling practice, I work with clients of all ages who struggle with various forms of FOMO, so often exacerbated by the unbridled mental chatter of "compare and contrast." For example, a client well into her thirties wants so much to get married and have children, and yet has not been able to find a potential partner or spouse despite putting forth considerable time and effort on numerous online dating sites. This is difficult enough to deal with, but is made even more painful when she enters the world of social media, for example Facebook, Instagram, and/or Twitter, only to discover the joyful news of yet another acquaintance or friend who, unlike her, has recently become engaged. Another client, a recent college graduate, has only been able to find part-time employment so far, and not even remotely in his field of study, which in his mind does not look so good when he compares himself, by way of social networking, with other classmates already more gainfully employed. Finally, a middle-aged mother is trying to set healthier boundaries for herself when it comes to perusing social media sites, for so often her initial intention of simply getting caught up with all the wonderful things other friends are doing with their children quickly morphs into a guilty and hopeless feeling that she is not doing enough as a mother, that somehow she is missing out on the fleeting years she has with her children. In developing a theology of technology, as well as in the work of pastoral and spiritual care, it is important to keep in mind that the problem is not technology itself, but rather as Delio rightly suggests, what we as human beings do with it, what we expect of it, and how we will relate to it. If we relate to the digital technologies, in this particular case social media and networking, with anxious and vigilant awareness, afraid that if we do not we will inevitably be missing out on something of consequence, we are in effect keeping the stress region of our brain on high alert.

Whether technology becomes more opportunity or threat, or vice versa, will depend more on what we as human beings do with it, how we make use of it and how we relate to it, individually and collectively. It is therefore fundamentally a human problem, whether we are putting digital technologies to good use or not for ourselves as individuals, and on a much greater scale if we are doing so collectively on behalf of human society. We have noted remarkable advances in AI-based healthcare and AI-assistive technologies, such as human implants and enhancements designed to improve if not restore hearing, vision, cognitive and memory function, and bodily movement and coordination. This is certainly putting technology to good use for human individuals and society as a whole, restoring the quality of life for so many people. At the same time, a closer look at the development of these AI technologies reveals a potential downside or threat, if they are not guided toward loving and just ends with *all* people in mind. Historically, medical practitioners have been guided by the well-known Hippocratic oath, which focuses first and foremost on the care and the treatment of sick individuals among us. Healing the sick has therefore been nothing short of an "egalitarian project," for the greater good of human society, "because it assumed that there is a normative standard of physical and mental health that everyone can and should enjoy" (Harari, 2017, p. 353). But in the digital age of powerful AI-based healthcare and human-enhancement technology, this historically noble and just approach to medicine could give way to something less egalitarian if we are not careful. "The expectation that this process will be repeated in the twenty-first century may be just wishful thinking," given that "twenty-first-century medicine is increasingly aiming to upgrade the healthy" (Harari, 2017, p. 353).

This is fundamentally a justice issue, which pastoral and practical theologians and pastoral and spiritual practitioners will want to, *need* to reflect on immediately. From a theological standpoint, it is a most unsettling development, for it would mean that medicine in general and human-enhancement technology in particular will become less of an egalitarian project, and instead be used primarily in the service of those possessing the financial means to "upgrade." This is not only about the distribution of money and wealth, or the lack thereof, that a small percentage of us will have plenty of it to spend on the latest enhancement technologies while others of us, the vast majority, are just trying to maintain the most basic healthcare. Put another way, "the concern is not simply that the wealthy may be able to buy something that the poor cannot afford, but also that by purchasing enhancement technology, the wealthy might in turn convert their present wealth into future power, thereby widening the social gap between the few who are enhanced and the many who remain merely natural" (Cole-Turner, 2011b, p. 194). The greater challenge, in other words, will be how well we as a society can manage human greed and power, and whether we can help guide enhancement technologies toward more just and equitable ends. Otherwise, medicine will fast become less about the egalitarian care and treatment of the sick, as it has been for millennia, and more about upgrading the healthiest among us:

> Upgrading the healthy is an elitist project, because it rejects the idea of a universal standard applicable to all and seeks to give some individuals an edge over others. People want superior memories, above-average intelligence, and first-class sexual abilities. If some form of upgrade becomes so cheap and common that everyone enjoys it, it will simply be considered the new baseline, which the next generation of treatments will strive to surpass . . . the poor could very well enjoy much better healthcare than today, but the gap separating them from the rich will nevertheless be much greater. (Harari, 2017, p. 353)

We cannot passively assume that we will automatically guide the development of human-enhancement technology, and with it the coming merger of humans and machines toward just and egalitarian ends, given our track record historically and even at present. We have so often taken the biblical mandate to "have dominion" over the earth (Genesis 1:26–28) to extremes, so much so that scientists are now warning that the planet is on the verge of, in the words of the title of a study published in the journal, *Proceedings of the National Academy of Sciences* (Ceballos *et al.*, 2017), "biological annihilation via the ongoing sixth mass extinction," with the "ultimate drivers" of the biotic destruction being, not surprisingly, "human overpopulation and continued population growth, and overconsumption, especially by the rich." Scientists refer to the present epoch of the planet as the Holocene, and "yet it may be better to call the last 70,000 years the Anthropocene epoch: the epoch of humanity" (Harari, 2017, p. 72). In a relatively brief period of time, when viewed in the context of earth's vast history, human beings have become "the single most important agent of change in the global ecology," to the extent that "our impact is already on a par with that of ice ages and tectonic movements" (Harari, 2017, pp. 72–73). The brunt of the impact has put the planet at acute risk, given the findings published in the highly respected journal of the National Academy of Sciences. Indeed, it is remarkable if not lamentable that "within a century, our impact may surpass that of the asteroid that killed off the dinosaurs 65 million years ago," so that "instead of fearing asteroids, we should fear ourselves" (Harari, 2017, p. 73).

The view of perpetual human progress, that we are ever moving onward and upward, stands in urgent need of reassessment in light of the unprecedented and daunting challenges before us, some of which are of our own making. A theology of technology must therefore be grounded in the pressing realities of the present moment, if it is not to become yet another abstraction dissociated from the actual lived and embodied experience of human beings. Nor can it assume that we will somehow find a way to guide the evolutionary merger of humans and machines toward just and charitable ends, given the present and complicated state of human nature and the so-called human condition. If we put it in theological language, we can say that "while the human condition may be characterized in different ways, depending on the specific doctrinal system—such as suffering, limitation, sinfulness, illusion, separation, ignorance, rebirth, brokenness, or some combination of these—the conviction is that something is bad and needs to change" (Hopkins, 2015, p. 71). There is, then, the need for a reality check:

> Homo sapiens are the latest arrival in the evolutionary story, the most complex and intelligent species and, yet, the most unnatural species alive. We separate ourselves from the whole and refuse to be part of the whole; we kill and maim our own species, as well as other species. We lock ourselves up in artificial environments with artificial lighting and sit behind artificial computer screens, sometimes creating artificial lives online because our own lives are so boring and empty. We boast of our intelligence as human creatures but we have lost the human center that feels for another, that weeps for the poor and oppressed, that has a righteous anger in the face of injustice, that forgives our enemies and shows mercy to the wounded. Being created for wholeness in love we are the most loveless of creatures filled with fear, jealousy, anger, hurt, resistance, and rivalry. A center empty of love is ripe for extinction because there is nothing to live for. (Delio, 2013, pp. 180–181)

We do well not to lose sight of the present and complicated state of human nature, even as we aspire to help guide the development of technology toward just and hopeful ends for human individuals and for human society as a whole, indeed help guide our increasing merger with intelligent machines. The need for in-depth theological reflection, *now* rather than later, is obvious, for when the merger is more complete and machine learning has achieved artificial general (human-level) intelligence, time will no longer be on our side. By then, AI will be poised to surpass human intelligence, on its way to achieving artificial superintelligence, and we will have become more Techno than Homo sapiens. This assumes that we can be more realistic and less grandiose about any view of human progress, given the state of human nature and the human condition, and about the extent of our capacity to helpfully guide the present evolutionary transition forward. Whether the further development of machine intelligence is more opportunity than threat, or the reverse, is less about technology in and of itself and more about the complicated state of human nature. Will we, say thirty or fifty or a hundred years from now, look back and conclude that the human capacity for compassion and justice was at the forefront of helping to guide technological development, or will it be the opposite, our capacity for power, greed, and profit that guided the process less benevolently? Perhaps more fundamentally, we are not even remotely clear about what it means to be witnessing the rapid and exponential advance of computer intelligence, for as Bostrom (2016) has argued, it is "a challenge for which we are not ready now and will not be ready for a long time" (p. 319). Ready or not, however, technology will not be slowing down anytime soon, if ever, waiting for us to catch up. "Before the prospect of an intelligence explosion, we humans are like small children playing with a bomb," for "such is the mismatch between the power of our plaything and the immaturity of our conduct" (Bostrom, 2016, p. 319). As we noted in the previous chapter, in a digital age we are in so many ways in over our heads, and yet we still have a window of time and opportunity before we witness the full "explosion" of machine intelligence. "We have," notes Bostrom (2016), "little idea when the detonation will occur, though if we hold the device to our ear we can hear a faint ticking sound" (p. 319).

Chapter Three

Human Nature and Technological Enhancement

As we are already in the midst of a major *and* unprecedented evolutionary transition, with biology merging with technology, it is not too soon to be asking, how will this change our understanding of human nature, particularly as we continue to align with machines and therefore become more technologically constituted? Put more simply, what will it mean to be *human* when technology has more completely fused with biology in the human person? Will human beings still be a reflection of the divine image, of the *imago Dei*, when we have become more Techno than Homo sapiens? The fusion of biology and technology is well underway, as we have seen in previous chapters, and we are increasingly beyond the point of no return. There has never been, nor will there ever be, any going back when it comes to the evolutionary process, so as technology becomes more of the dominant driving force in that process, its fusion with biology is becoming irreversible. Even now, ahead of any technological singularity, "we spend the majority of our waking time communicating through digitally-mediated channels; it is common practice to convert deaf children into functional cyborgs using cochlear implants; we trust artificial intelligence with our lives through anti-braking in cars and autopilots in planes; most transactions on the stock market are executed by automated trading algorithms; and our electric grids are in the hands of artificial intelligence" (Gillings *et al.*, 2016, pp. 10–11). And, remarkably all of it has happened in a matter of a few decades, in no time at all when situated within the historically long and arduous process of evolution and the development of organic life. The authors of the peer-reviewed article, "Information in the Biosphere: Biological and Digital Worlds," published in the journal, *Trends in Ecology and Evolution*, help us put this in sharper focus, leaving no doubt that given its accelerated reach and power, technology will only continue to reshape and perhaps ultimately transform the entire evolutionary process, including human life as we have known it. They write:

> The accumulation of digital information is happening at an unprecedented speed. After RNA genomes were replaced with DNA, it then took a billion years for eukaryotes to appear, and roughly another two billion for multicellular organisms with a nervous system. It took another 500 million years to develop neural systems capable of forming languages. From there, it took only 100,000 years to develop written language, and a further 4,500 years before the invention of printing presses capable of rapid replication of this written information. The digitalization of the entire stockpile of technologically-mediated information has taken less than 30 years. Less than one percent of information was in digital format in the mid-1980s, growing to more than 99% today. (Gillings *et al.*, 2016, pp. 10–11)

BECOMING "BORGED"

Digital technologies have come upon us with astonishing speed and force, in the blink of an eye when viewed evolutionarily; they are nothing short of, to put it colloquially, a "game-changer." For billions of years, the evolutionary process has been confined to the realm of organic life, but now it is breaking out at light speed into the vastness of the inorganic realm. Technology is rapidly merging with biology, as is machine intelligence with human intelligence, so that the symbiosis between the biological and the digital, between the organic and the inorganic could very well "sidestep the slow pace of natural selection and evolution" (Gillings *et al.*, 2016, p. 11). The issue of human identity, of what constitutes human nature in an age of increasing biological-technological hybridity, must now become a central focus of our theological and psychological reflection and discourse, not simply another issue among many others. "The influx of technology," writes Delio (2008), "into our daily life is transforming our patterns of play, work, love, birth, sickness, and death," so that we are fast becoming, to use her word, "borged" (p. 162). For example, "an increasing number of people are becoming 'cyborged' in a technical sense, including people with electronic pacemakers, artificial joints, drug implant systems, implanted corneal lenses, and artificial skin" (Delio, 2008, p. 162). This reflects, as we have noted in earlier chapters, the extraordinary advances in medical technology and AI-based healthcare, which has dramatically enhanced the quality of life for so many people. Notwithstanding the recent and amazing advances in medicine, it does not quite capture the bigger picture, specifically technology's powerful impact on *all of us*, on human life in general. If we have not become literal cyborgs by way of human implant and enhancement technologies, we are still active participants in a digital culture, making many of us at the very least into "metaphoric cyborgs" (Delio, 2008, p. 162): the video gamer, for example, who spends the vast majority of his waking life in the gaming world of virtual reality; the college student who is always cybernetically connected to one or more of her digital "screens," so that she does not miss out on anything (FOMO); and the parent who cannot seem to get through the day or even the hour for that matter without the help and support of this or that digital assistant.

All of this raises some very important and rather profound questions about human identity and human nature, in light of technology's growing reach and impact: Who are we becoming as a species? What are we becoming? What have we already become, as literal and/or metaphoric cyborgs? And, what will we become when we are no longer strictly Homo sapiens anymore, when the merger of humans and machines is more complete and we have entered a world of post-biological evolution? The integration of technology in human life, as Delio (2008) suggested earlier, is now of such degree that we must consider very seriously the possibility that we are *already* transitioning into Techno sapiens. She extends her reflection further, putting it in even more vivid terms: "Biological evolution and technological evolution have become co-terminus, and a new posthuman species is emerging" (Delio, 2013, p. 159). Put another way, we could say that a new post-Homo sapiens species is already starting to emerge. For some of us who hold to a more static theological framework, viewing God and the world and humanity as more or less changeless and/or fixed, it could be enough of a challenge to get our minds around the possibility that human beings are already transitioning from Homo to Techno sapiens, without even pondering the possibility that this will result in the emergence of a *posthuman* species. And yet, as we have seen, divine nature according to the prophet (Isaiah 43:19) is anything but static, for God is forever doing a new thing in the world *and* with human beings. Interestingly, the various branches of contemporary science, including cosmology, quantum physics, and machine learning would all in a way seem to corroborate the ancient wisdom of the prophetic words, that there is and always will be a fundamental dynamism inherent to life and the world, which reflects a dynamic divine and by extension human nature. As for our own human nature, it is very important that we keep in mind that it has never been fixed and stationary; "it has always been evolving, but what was once a crawl has accelerated" (Green, 2015, p. 206).

The accelerated evolution of human nature is of course due to the impact of technology, and the momentous advances that are occurring in the field of machine intelligence. As we have noted, what has most surprised the scientific researchers themselves, working on the front lines of AI research, is not that machine intelligence continues to evolve but rather the *speed* with which it is doing so. In a way, the same can be said for human nature, for if in fact a rapidly developing technology has become the central organizing force in the evolutionary process, and we are already beginning to merge with it, then we can expect human nature to be evolving and changing commensurately. Recall that the human brain has always been most skillful at adapting to any and every environment, so that as our present digital environment continues changing in dramatic and unprecedented ways, the brain by its very nature will be adapting and changing with it in equally unprecedented ways. There is, however, one important qualification: for millennia the biological brain has been adapting to changing circumstances in the same *organic* realm, whereas it must now find a way of adapting to something qualitatively different, namely the digital world and the vastness of the *inorganic* realm. And, for all the marvels of the biological brain, it is no match for the potency of today's emerging digital technologies. "As advances in information technology and communication supply us with information at an ever-accelerating rate, the limitations of our brains become all the more obvious" (Klingberg, 2009, p. 3).

It is more than a little sobering to learn that the brain we have today is little changed, genetically, from what it was tens of thousands of years ago. While it has been and continues to be an adaptation machine extraordinaire, the similarities between the Cro-Magnon brain of forty thousand years ago and the brain we have today are by far greater than the differences (Klingberg, 2009, p. 85). The same brain now has to take on the torrent of information that is discharged by a digital society, and there are strong indications that it is finding it more challenging to absorb let alone process the informational bombardment. Part of the challenge may have to do with the fact that it is encased within a physical cranium, which imposes an infrastructural limitation on any future development. There are, in other words, "energy and infrastructural constraints that ultimately govern human brain size and activity," so that "our brain size may be approaching the evolutionary limits of cognitive power" (Gillings *et al.*, 2016, p. 11). To be clear, the evolutionary constraint is *biological* in nature, so that if there is a limitation to cognitive power it is within the brain of Homo sapiens. The brain of Techno sapiens, however, may not have the same constraints and limitations, for in the increasing merger with machine intelligence we will be entering the vastness of the digital world, a non-biological realm that is not governed by the same biological laws of nature.

At first glance, this might appear to be little more than a direct threat to human nature, to that which has made us uniquely human for millennia, and to a certain extent it is a threat to our very own nature as Homo sapiens. But what about our evolving nature as Techno sapiens; might this also be something of an opportunity, notwithstanding our apprehension and fear? If the human brain is hitting the wall, so to speak, with infrastructural limitations and therefore with further cognitive development, then it could very well be in our own best interests to intentionally help guide the merger of human and machine intelligence toward more expansive and less confined ends. "Given that physical restrictions may prevent evolutionary improvements in cognition, the integration of biological with digital processing and information storage is one way forward" (Gillings *et al.*, 2016, p. 11). Biological evolution will continue to unfold at its own methodical pace, to take nothing away from it, governed by physical constraints and limitations, whereas the evolution of AI knows no such limitations. In fact, from all indications it appears that the development of technology is becoming super-exponential: "new computational platforms, from nano-technological modeling of neurons, to developments in quantum computing, provide justification that artificial processing might maintain its exponential growth even beyond its silicon basis" (Gillings *et al.*, 2016, p. 11). As we continue merging with these evolving digital technologies, there is the distinct possibility that we will eventually surmount the biological limitations of cognitive power, by learning to enhance brain functioning associated with certain neural regions, in particular those involved with higher-order thinking. For example, in the area of higher-level cognition, "it might be possible to enlarge the pre-frontal cortex, simply by adding to its neuron count," for in a computer simulation it would not be confined by the physical limitations of the cranium (Shanahan, 2015, p. 94).

As we become more technologically enhanced human beings, the issue of human identity and what constitutes human nature in a digital world will demand our ongoing attention and reflection. We have suggested that we are on the way to becoming an enhanced species of Techno sapiens, at the very least metaphoric cyborgs that can no longer be considered strictly Homo sapiens in the traditional sense. As biological evolution and technological evolution become more and more co-terminus and intertwined, we will have to consider the possibility that we have started evolving into a posthuman species, with profound implications for our theological reflection and more practically for the work of pastoral and spiritual care. "The technologies of human enhancement raise a puzzling question about the transformation of the human individual: Is the enhanced person still the same person" (Cole-Turner, 2011a, p. 10)? My own father, for example, following the surgical insertion of a cochlear implant chip, is still to a certain extent the same person, but in another way he is not, now that he is quite literally a technologically enhanced person. Without the implant, he would still have only a tiny percentage of his hearing, continuing to miss out on so much of the conversation with friends and family, not to mention the familiar sounds of songbirds that he is hearing once again after so many years. So, does it really matter if the technologically enhanced client or congregant is still the "same person" or not, when the tangible benefit is that he or she can now experience life more abundantly? But as the technologies of enhancement move further into the area of brain emulation and mind uploading, we will have to ponder an even more profound question having to do with, not only the human individual, but with "the transformation of the human species: Is the enhanced person still human?" Cole-Turner (2011a) rhetorically invites us to walk a fine line between the potential threat *and* opportunity:

> Some believe that given enough time, technology will modify human beings so much that they will no longer be human in the usual sense but will have become some other species of hominid. If this were to happen, would it amount to a kind of species suicide, the death of human nature as evolved and as we have always known it? And if so, would this be a step of technologically sophisticated lunacy, something akin, say to a mass exchange of nuclear weapons? Or is there something deep in evolution itself that drives us forward in this direction so that we would have to regard such a step as comparable to the evolution of conscious or self-conscious beings? (p. 10)

If we put the last question of the above quote in even more theological language, we could ask similarly and again rhetorically, is there something deep in *creation* and the divine nature that is moving forward the transformation of the human species, from self-conscious Homo sapiens to technologically enhanced Techno sapiens, and perhaps eventually leading to the emergence of a completely new being with superintelligent capabilities? The image of God, as we discussed in the previous chapter, is a constant call forward, ever moving us and all of creation into the vast and profound mystery of the future, whether we are fully ready or not. Our response to this dynamic divine energy and creativity is, as Rahner suggests, a pure openness to absolutely everything, so that we are able to find God in all things and therefore help guide the unprecedented change unfolding before us toward just and hopeful ends. It is, in other words, a pre-apprehension of the divine presence in the existential opportunity of the present moment, as we witness the increasing merger of humans with machines and an emerging biological-technological hybridity. If we can step outside of our own anthropocentric thinking long enough to embrace a more expansive cosmological perspective, we will see that at the very least there is the *possibility* that the emergence of Techno sapiens reflects the divine call forward into the vastness of the future. To regard our increasing merger with technology as not only a threat but also a potential existential opportunity, reflects a more spacious cosmological view, a pure openness for absolutely everything that is at bottom a pre-apprehension of the dynamic and infinite divine presence. As Rahner (1986) put it so well toward the end of his life, with important implications for theological reflection in a digital age:

> The true system of thought really is the knowledge that humanity is finally directed precisely not toward what it can control in knowledge but toward the absolute mystery as such; that mystery is not just an unfortunate remainder of what is not yet known but rather the blessed goal of knowledge which comes to itself when it is with the incomprehensible one, and not in any other way. In

other words, then, the system is the system of what cannot be systematized. (pp. 196–197)

THE WOBBLINESS OF HUMAN PROGRESS

It is important to make clear that this is not a romanticizing of the present digital age, as if the emerging technologies, such as artificial intelligence, will become something of a "savior," guiding us ever onward and upward into the future. Any idea or theory of human progress applied to Homo and/ or Techno sapiens must be viewed with a healthy hermeneutic of suspicion, given the human historical record over time and even recently. Whether the merger of human and machine intelligence occurs in thirty years or fifty years or longer, we can fully expect that between now and then and even thereafter, it will be, in the words of scientist James Lovelock (2016), "a rough ride to the future." As we noted earlier, technology is very much a double-edged sword, on the one hand posing an unprecedented existential risk to humanity, but on the other hand dramatically enhancing the quality of life for so many people. "As exciting as this technology is, with great potential for good, it also has the potential to disrupt society as we know it today" (Hendler & Mulvehill, 2016, p. 11). In fact, the disruption and transformation of human society has already begun, as we become increasingly "borged." And yet, whether technology ultimately becomes more opportunity than threat, or unsettlingly the opposite, depends less on the digital technologies and much more on what we as human beings decide to do with them. The challenge or problem before us, as we discussed in the previous chapter, is fundamentally less technological and more *human* in nature, specifically the problem of an unpredictable and at times erratic human nature. We cannot simply assume, given the human track record, that we will help guide the future development and application of technology toward the greater good of human society. We would do well to keep in mind that a mere hundred and fifty years ago, just "yesterday" or more likely still "today" when it comes to evolutionary time, "slavery still was widely practiced in the American south, with full support of the law and moral custom" (Bostrom, 2016, p. 257). More recently, white supremacy and nationalism has reared its ugly head again in America and throughout the world, as if nothing has changed in the human heart and mind, despite our lofty moral aspirations. Though we have certainly gleaned a certain amount of moral insight along the way, "we could hardly claim to be now basking in the high noon of perfect moral enlightenment" (Bostrom, 2016, p. 257).

The implication is that we cannot romanticize or overvalue human nature either, as well as biological intelligence for that matter, as if we are further along the path toward enlightenment than is really the case, with little need of any assistance from technology. Some are saying that the resurgence of racism and white supremacy, in America for example, is merely a "step backward" in the overall trajectory toward progressive moral enlightenment in general and racial progress in particular. We cannot assume that it is really this simple, as if America's "messiness," past and present, reflects "a single historical force taking steps forward and backward on race" (Kendi, 2017). The historian, Ibram Kendi (2017), thinks it is far more complex and multidimensional, rhetorically asking in a *New York Times* Op-Ed article, "But what if there have been *two* historical forces at work: a dual and dueling history of racial progress and the simultaneous progression of racism?" The presidential election of 2016, and the subsequent in-your-face marches for white supremacy, nationalism, and separatism, without any hoods or masks, would therefore not represent so much a step backward for racial progress but rather on a completely different dueling track and trajectory more of a step *forward* for racism and our deep racial divisions. "We can no longer," writes Kendi (2017), "parade the exceptional twin, and try to hide away the other history," all the while clinging to the illusion of American progress and, more broadly, human exceptionalism. Whether we see the resurgence of racial and ethnic hatred in America, as well in many other regions of the world, as simply a step backward in the long and progressive human march toward equality and justice for all, or like Kendi (2017) as a step forward for the unexceptional and perverse "twin" of racist progress, the fact is that in either case it will continue to be a rough and bumpy ride into the future for human beings and for biological life and intelligence.

This is not at all meant to downplay or minimize what President Lincoln referred to famously as the "better angels" of our human nature, which we have so often put to good use in the ongoing and arduous quest for social justice and equality, among many other noble endeavors. At the same time, it is necessary to urge caution when it comes to an uncritical embrace of human exceptionalism and progress, for as it turns out human nature is also something of a double-edged sword, much like the digital technologies we have been discussing, inherently posing both an opportunity *and* threat, in this case to the planet, other species, and even ourselves. A reality check is therefore in order for those of us who hold an overly idealistic view of human life and nature, who feel quite confident that given enough time we will figure it out, as we progressively move closer and closer toward moral enlightenment. But if we idealize human nature, particularly a biological understanding of it, we make it rather difficult to even consider the possibility of an emerging biological-technological hybridity, for as the thinking goes it would be a violation of the sacred order of things and even of natural law. But would it necessarily be a violation of the sacred order? Perhaps it is if God is *not* doing anything new; however, if in fact God *is* doing something new, and who of us can ever say "no" definitively, then the pre-apprehension of divine presence in this momentous time would lead us to conclude that there is at least a *possibility* that it is not a violation, that it is as much existential opportunity as it is threat and perhaps even more. We can only hope that God is still doing a new thing in the world and with human beings, given the double-edgedness of human nature and the limitations of our cognitive and moral development. Nick Bostrom (2016) wonders, intriguingly, if ultimately "moral goodness might be more of a precious metal than an abundant element in human nature" (p. 267), despite our lofty hopes that it is there in greater abundance. He notes that this would help explain "the tardiness and wobbliness of humanity's progress on many of the 'eternal problems,'" which would likely reflect the limitations of an evolving human cortex (Bostrom, 2016, pp. 7).

I want to be very clear that I am in no way trying to denigrate human nature, somehow suggesting that we are fundamentally flawed and as such beyond all hope. Nor am I even hinting at any original sinfulness per se, unless we are reframing this theology in a way that contextualizes it within the present study of neuroscience and evolutionary science. For any theology of original sin, and by extension any theology of sinful human nature to have relevance for the present day and age, it will need to be reframed in a way that what we as human beings are confessing is not so much "a deep remorse for any innate flaw or defect but rather a mindful and realistic awareness of our collective development at this particular stage of human history" (Bingaman, 2014, pp. 51–52). To point out the obvious, human beings still have a very long way to go on the developmental and evolutionary spectrum, which reflects the present limitations of the human cortex, the neural region of our higher-order thinking and executive functioning. "This state of affairs," the renowned neuroscientist Joseph LeDoux (2002) has observed, "is part of the price we pay for having newly evolved cognitive capacities that are not yet fully integrated into our brains" (p. 322). In other words, the higher-order cortical areas of human thinking and reasoning are a more recent evolutionary development, when compared to the much older and deeply ingrained limbic areas of fear and aggression. But having a long way to go, evolutionarily, would appear to be applicable not only to human beings but to biological life and to the natural world in general, particularly if we view it from the perspective of a more just and peaceable world. In terms of the natural world, as beautiful as it is and as much as I am drawn to it personally, the total amount of suffering in it per year is, in the words of evolutionary biologist Richard Dawkins (1995), "beyond all decent contemplation" (p. 132). Quite literally in any given moment, "thousands of animals are being eaten alive, others are running for their lives, whimpering with fear, others are being slowly devoured from within by rasping parasites, thousands of all kinds are dying of starvation, thirst, and disease" (Dawkins, 1995, p. 132). To this, Bostrom (2016) adds the following:

> Even just within our species, 150,000 persons are destroyed each day while countless more suffer an appalling array of torments and deprivations. Nature might be a great experimentalist, but one who would never pass muster with an ethics review board—contravening the Helsinki Declaration and every norm of moral decency, left, right, and center. It is important that we not gratuitously replicate such horrors *in silico*. Mind crime seems especially difficult to avoid when evolutionary methods are used to produce human-like intelligence, at least if the process is meant to look anything like actual biological evolution. (p. 230)

We can only wonder the extent to which we are able to endow machine intelligence with a moral or ethical sense, the extent to which we can guide the process toward just and loving ends when our own cognitive and moral development is still very much a work in progress. Indeed, just trying to define "moral rightness" for ourselves has occupied philosophers and theologians for millennia, still occupies them, with no apparent agreement in sight anytime soon that would unite us as a species in global accord. The notion of "morally right," in other words, is "a notoriously difficult concept, one with which philosophers have grappled since antiquity without yet attaining consensus to its analysis" (Bostrom, 2016, p. 267). Once again, this is less a reflection of a defective or even sinful human nature, and more the price we pay as a biological species for having, relatively speaking, only recently evolved cognitive capacities that are far from being fully integrated into our brains. Whereas the earlier-evolved limbic circuitry connected to fear and aggression is more deeply rooted in our human physiology, going further down the brain stem and even further, down into the central nervous system (CNS), our higher-order cognitive circuitry is located, as it were, higher up in the outermost layers of the brain, reflecting a more recent evolutionary development. We can only imagine what the human species will become in time, as our capacity for higher-order thinking and executive functioning is more fully integrated into the human brain. This assumes that we will continue to follow a similar evolutionary path, one that it is still primarily biological in nature, which means that it will be a rather long and extended period of time before our higher cortical functions are more fully integrated into the brain. But what if we do not continue to follow a similar path? There is, as we have been discussing, a very distinct possibility that with the increasing merger of humans with machines, we may not have to wait so long. If and when we arrive at the technological singularity, our higher-order thinking and cortical functioning will quickly move to the fast track. Whether this occurs in thirty years or a hundred years from now, it is all the same if we adopt a cosmological point of view, for in either case it is merely a blip in time.

Herein lies the conundrum, particularly if we are determined to preserve at all costs a biocentric view of human life and nature: if we could somehow manage to bypass technology, if this were even possible, and continue our evolution primarily on a biological path, we can expect it to be a *very* long time before our higher-order cognitive capacities are more fully integrated into the brain. The rhetorical question then becomes, do we have that kind of time anymore, if in fact we have reached a tipping point for human life and for life in general on the planet, with the risk of biological annihilation looming? In all likelihood it is a moot point anyway, for as we have already seen technology, with its accelerated and powerful advance, has moved to the front of the line as the primary driving force guiding the evolutionary process. Thus, given the dramatic differential between the rate of evolutionary change for technology and for that of human biology, it would appear as if the door is swiftly closing, if it has not closed already, on a path that is exclusively or even primarily biological in nature. At the very least, there is a biological-technological hybridity emerging, if not the early signs of a new species, Homo sapiens transitioning to Techno sapiens. If so, there is the possibility that we might be better poised as *Techno* sapiens to deal with the challenges of "life at the tipping point," with our cognitive capacities technologically enhanced and upgraded. Even so, it will still be challenging for some of us to accept that human life and nature will never be the same again, that it might even be a violation of the sacred order of creation and of the natural order of things. As Tamar Sharon (2014) has noted, "what is at stake here is human nature . . . the *givenness* of human nature can be seen as the defining characteristic, or fundamental essence, of what it means to be human in this perspective" (p. 3). Therefore, in partnering with technology to enhance our cognitive capabilities, as exciting and even useful as this might be, the risk in intervening or "tampering" with our own human nature is that we are potentially "playing God." The fact that we are born and die, and in between those two realities we live *and* struggle and suffer along the way, is simply the way it is preordained for human beings and all of life in the context of the natural order, or so the thinking goes with this theological perspective. "Technological intervention, at least for enhancement purposes, poses a threat to human nature and the values and virtues that humans have developed as a result of the necessity to deal with the imperfection inherent to this nature" (Sharon, 2014, p. 3).

It is indeed worth reflecting on the values that we have developed over time to deal with the inherent virtues and limitations of our own human nature, while there is still a window of time and opportunity to do so, *before* the merger of human and machine intelligence is more fully upon us. There is still time, in other words, to preserve the very best of human nature, what has made and continues to make us uniquely human, to determine how life can still be lived as much as possible on our own *human* terms. The moment to still take matters into our own hands, to cultivate certain human virtues such as our capacity for attentional control and mindful awareness, remains before us, but the window could be fast closing with the rapid advance of digital technologies. With technology becoming the more powerful and dominant driving force of the evolutionary process, the challenge will be, if it is not already, cultivating attentional stability, sustained concentration, and meaningful contemplative living. I will have more to say about this in coming chapters. It is also worth preserving as much as we possibly can the extraordinary virtue of consciousness, *human* consciousness, even if intelligence is in the process of decoupling from it. For all we know, consciousness could very well be something utterly unique, as far as the universe and even our own Milky Way galaxy is concerned. "We take for granted that we are conscious, but we do not understand the long, torturous sequence of biological events that have transpired to make this possible" (Kaku, 2014, p. 327). It has led the cognitive scientist, Steven Pinker (2007), to conclude, with language that is rather spiritual if not theological, that "nothing gives life more purpose than the realization that every moment of consciousness is a precious and fragile gift." Human consciousness, and this is not at all hyperbole, is nothing short of miraculous when considered within the vastness of cosmic time and space. The "miracle" as it were is not, as some would say, that it suddenly appeared out of nowhere in a split-second, but rather that consciousness has been a far more complex and circuitous evolutionary process. It is, to be sure, a most precious and fragile gift, something to be preserved and nurtured in the midst of a digital age, while we still have time before machine learning achieves human-level intelligence. The paradox, as Paul Ricoeur (1991) has observed, is that on a cosmic scale human life, both individually and collectively as a species, is "insignificant," and yet "this brief period of time when we appear in the world is the moment during which all meaningful questions arise" (p. 343).

IMAGO DEI AND TECHNOLOGICALLY ENHANCED HUMANS

Before moving on to discuss the preservation and cultivation of certain human virtues and attributes, such as conscious and compassionate awareness, attentional control, and in-depth reflection, there is another important issue that we must first explore, having to do with the impact of technology and machine intelligence on human nature: Are technologically enhanced human beings, not to mention Techno sapiens, still a reflection of the *imago Dei*, the divine image of God? Or, when we more fully make the transition from Homo to Techno sapiens, post-technological singularity, will that signal the end of us having anything to do with *imago Dei*? Even now, before any singularity has occurred, before there is the emergence of artificial general intelligence (AGI) and the more complete merger of humans and machines, it is still worth asking: To what extent are we *today* a reflection of *imago Dei*, in the traditional sense of the term and the theology, if as Ilia Delio (2008) has suggested the integration of technology in human life is already of such degree that we must consider the possibility of being at least in the early stages of Techno sapiens? At the very least, we reflect along with the divine image an increasing biological-technological hybridity, which begs another and even more profound question: Are we the manifestation of a threefold merger taking place between biology, technology, *and* divinity? It is certainly worth considering, in fact necessary for us to consider, given that we are beyond the point of no return. Technology is now the more powerful force driving the evolutionary process, more dominant than biology, for unlike the long, circuitous, and oftentimes "tortuous" route of biological evolution over billions of years, the evolution of technology is occurring at near light speed, in a matter of a few decades. Therefore, notwithstanding the marvels of biological evolution, and there are many, biology cannot even remotely begin to keep up with the exponential advance and proliferation of digital technologies. And, as we learned earlier, it will only continue at an increasing accelerated rate, due in large measure to Moore's law and beyond that to the emergence of quantum and optical computing. Keeping all of this in mind, we can conclude that the threefold merger of biology, technology, *and* divinity is not at all beyond the realm of possibility, nor is the idea that technologically enhanced humans will soon begin to reflect a more complex divine image.

Ilia Delio has already argued convincingly that our theological reflection must move beyond a surface understanding of the role of technology in today's world, beyond seeing it as one issue among many others, something external to us that we are having to deal with. This fails to grasp the more profound and powerful reach of technology, that it is now central and integral to the whole evolutionary process, to the evolution of human beings, driving us toward new levels of complexity and consciousness. Given its powerful advance and reach, again in virtually no time at all when viewed evolutionarily, we can begin to see without too much difficulty that we are on an irreversible course. It is interesting to note that as far back as the mid-1970s, well before the Internet and World Wide Web were introduced, the famed computer scientist and MIT researcher, Joseph Weizenbaum (1976), was already discussing the idea of "irreversibility," a central feature of the evolutionary process, in the context of the development of computers. "Some human actions," he wrote, "the introduction of computers into some complex human activities, may constitute an irreversible commitment" (p. 28). Looking back more than forty years later, this is something of an understatement, even with his insight and prescience about the future. Evolution is inherently an irreversible process, so that as computer technology moves further and further into the "driver seat" of the evolutionary process, there is no reversing course. Weizenbaum (1976) adds, "the computer becomes an indispensable component of any structure once it is so thoroughly integrated with the structure, so enmeshed in various vital substructures, that it can no longer be factored out without fatally impairing the whole structure." He continues:

> It is not true that the American banking system or the stock and commodity markets or the great manufacturing enterprises would have collapsed had the computer not come along "just in time." It is true that the specific way in which these systems actually developed in the past two decades, and are still developing, would have been impossible without the computer. It is true that, were all the computers to suddenly disappear, much of the modern industrial-ized and militarized world would be thrown into great confusion and possibly utter chaos. The computer was not a prerequisite to the survival of modern society in the post-war period and beyond; its enthusiastic, uncritical embrace by the most "progressive" elements of American government, business, and industry quickly made it a resource essential to society's survival *in the form* that the computer itself had been instrumental in shaping. (pp. 28–29)

If we did not know any better, we would assume that Weizenbaum was commenting on recent developments of the present day and age, rather than the situation of over forty years ago. Even if we could hit the brakes, which is not possible, and put a stop to the accelerated advance of technology, it would lead to "utter chaos," to social and economic collapse on a global scale. It is necessary that we as pastoral and spiritual caregivers, clinical practitioners, and pastoral and practical theologians grasp the reality and import of the present situation, sooner rather than later, so that we do not invest precious time and energy and reflection trying to avoid the inevitable at all costs. From the perspective of mindfulness- and acceptance-based cog-nitive therapies, this would constitute a form of "experiential avoidance," which as we have learned in recent years is an obstacle to personal and collective growth and development. It is also an obstacle to the effective care of our clients and congregants living in a digital age, who need our help trying to navigate the new terrain in order to find, in Buddhist terms, the "middle path" between too much and too little technology, and between preserving what makes us uniquely human and accepting what we are be-coming. We can only accompany them, therapeutically, as far as we have navigated the terrain for ourselves, to the extent that we have learned to accept, more evenhandedly, the double-edged threat *and* opportunity of digi-tal technologies. "Acceptance," as we learned earlier, does not mean that we have to *like* everything about technology, or even technology at all for that matter. Rather, it is letting ourselves fully grasp and understand the double-edged impact of technology and machine intelligence on human development and human nature, that it is *already* becoming an irreversible game-changer. Moreover, it is letting ourselves consider the possibility that we as technolog-ically enhanced humans will ultimately reflect a more complex divine image, becoming the manifestation of a threefold merger between biology, technology, and divinity. In fact, the transformation has already begun, with evidence for an increasing biological-technological-spiritual hybridity.

This is not meant to brush aside or dismiss any narratives of apprehension, in particular theological narratives, which express real concern for the future of human life in a digital world. After all, technology is an unprecedented and complex cocktail of opportunity *and* threat, as Susan Greenfield (2015) has suggested, so that a healthy amount of caution is in order. If we put it in theological terms, it is balancing a hermeneutic of hope with a hermeneutic of suspicion, the latter rightly conveying the need to reflect very carefully on who we are as human beings and who we will become, in light of the *imago Dei*. For example, as we continue to reveal an increasing biological-technological-spiritual hybridity, further transitioning from Homo to Techno sapiens, will this either diminish or enhance the divine image within us? The truth is, it all depends. It could very well be diminished, *unless* we are proactively involved in helping to guide the process and our own evolution toward loving and wholesome ends, a reflection of the loving and creative nature of God. If we do not help guide the evolutionary process forward, if out of fear and apprehension we instead take a more passive and even hands-off approach, perhaps waiting for God to miraculously intervene to restore a former order that predates the arrival of computer technology or for God to reveal plain and simple the way forward, then we risk leaving so much of it to chance. And, this is something that we cannot afford to do, given the infinitely higher stakes for human life and human nature at present. To sit back and assume a passive posture, either in deference to an interventionist God or because we cannot accept the world of computer technology, i.e., we do not *like* it, leaves a precarious if not dangerous void that the "progressive elements" or power brokers of government, business, and finance, the "haves" in other words, are only too happy to fill *all by themselves*.

Something momentous is indeed occurring, as we find ourselves on the threshold of extraordinary change, approaching a decisive tipping point in the history of human life on the planet. Beyond it is uncharted territory, which as we traverse it will likely require an increasing amount of faith and hope in the goodness of God, the universe, and the whole evolutionary process. In a matter of only a few decades, we have witnessed scientific researchers in the field of computer technology and artificial intelligence turn a rather limited and unspectacular breakthrough into something far more world-shattering, with the potential to completely transform the very nature of life, the very nature of *human* life as we have known it. Some of us, however, may still be unmoved as we take a wait-and-see position, holding to the view that there really is not anything new under the sun, and that "this too shall pass." This would be a most unfortunate and serious mistake, for even now before we approach any sort of technological singularity, before we have transitioned from Homo to Techno sapiens, we are *already* seeing change that can only be described as *unprecedented*. True, we have not yet made any complete transition, but as Ilia Delio (2008) has rightly noted, we are already at an in-between evolutionary point between Homo sapiens proper and Techno sapiens, active participants in a digital culture that makes us even now into metaphoric cyborgs. In a way, it would be akin to the position that some of us are taking with atmospheric change and global warming, waiting to see how accurate the predictions of climate scientists will be before we take any action, before we step forward to help guide social policy toward more hopeful ends. Even if the scientific predictions of unrelenting climate change in coming years *only* partially come to pass, it will be a very different and challenging world for future generations. During the Holocene epoch of the past ten thousand years, earth's climate has been relatively stable, but as we move further into the Anthropocene epoch, the epoch of humanity, it is becoming less stable, exacerbated by a wait-and-see attitude. Similarly, if we adopt a wait-and-see position with computer technology and our merger with machines, then we have little if any chance to help guide the process toward just and hopeful ends, to help determine who we will become and how we will continue to reflect the divine image. Even if the "how" and "when" of an eventual human-machine merger continues to be debated, it is more than enough, as Murray Shanahan (2015) has argued convincingly, that there is a *significant probability* that we will witness the arrival of artificial superintelligence (ASI) sometime in the twenty-first century for it to command our immediate attention.

Between now and then, there is still a window of time and opportunity for us to develop an in-depth and evenhanded theology of technology, applying both a hermeneutic of suspicion *and* a hermeneutic of hope to the rise of digital technologies and artificial intelligence. In so doing, we are able to carefully reflect on who we are becoming as a species, who we *want* to become given the irreversible nature of technology and the whole evolutionary process, and how we intend to reflect the *imago Dei* as we increasingly become the manifestation of a threefold merger of biology, technology, and divinity. This assumes that humanity and all of life and the whole universe for that matter still have, so to speak, a long way to go, that the evolutionary process is far from reaching its end, if it ever will. In theological terms, it would mean that God is still doing a new thing with creation, even after billions of years and well before there were human beings on the face of the earth. If we can manage to step outside of our anthropocentric perspective and adopt a more cosmological point of view, long enough to begin grasping the "bigger picture," we will see that the whole cosmos is fundamentally and powerfully dynamic in nature. Thanks in large part to the Hubble telescope, only a very recent human invention, we now have a far better understanding of the vastness of the universe and the billions of galaxies, *each* with billions of stars, which are perpetually works in progress. At the other end of the spectrum, in the bizarre realm of subatomic particles, things are equally and maybe even more spectacularly dynamic if that is possible, as the findings from the CERN supercollider, the world's most powerful particle accelerator, have revealed. I mention this simply to reinforce the fact that the whole universe, including life on earth and with it human life, has been and will continue to be dynamically on a course of ever increasing complexity. As Murray Shanahan (2015) puts it, conveying a distinct cosmological perspective with important theological implications:

> Perhaps matter still has a long way to go on the scale of complexity. Perhaps there are forms of consciousness yet to arise that are, in some sense, superior to our own.
>
> Should we recoil from this prospect, or rejoice in it? Can we even make sense of such an idea? Whether or not the singularity is near, these are questions worth asking, not least because in attempting to answer them we shed light on ourselves and our place in the order of things. (pp. xxii–xxiii)

In developing a theology of technology, it is important to understand that our place in the order of things is fundamentally evolutionary and historical in nature, and that human personhood as well as human nature have never been, as we have been saying, fixed and stationary. The same is true for all of life on earth and in fact the whole universe, from the subatomic end of the spectrum to the cosmic. As human beings created *imago Dei*, we are therefore directed, as Karl Rahner (1986) has suggested, not so much toward what we *already* know and can control in our knowledge, but rather toward the pre-apprehension of what we do *not* know and what we cannot control, that is absolute mystery and infinite being. And, what we do not know about life, the universe, and our own human personhood and what we may eventually become as a species is considerable and vast. "The greatest scientific discovery," writes Harari (2017), "was the discovery of our ignorance," the moment when "humans realized how little they knew about the world" (p. 213). With our limited understanding of the world and universe, of ourselves as human beings, we would do well not to be exclusively invested in the familiar ways of knowing that we can control, but to also as Rahner (1986) urges, begin cultivating a pure openness for what cannot be systematized, infinite mystery and being. As we develop a more in-depth theology of technology and of artificial intelligence, Rahner's theology of *Vorgriff* offers us a way forward, for his "understanding of personhood is evolutionary in character and shares many parallels with the work of some thinkers in the field of emergence theory" (Fisher, 2015, p. 31). As such, it lends itself to our ongoing reflection about the present and future state of the human person in a digital world, already becoming a metaphoric cyborg and perhaps in the not-too-distant future further transitioning with all human beings into Techno sapiens. The evolutionary character of Rahner's (1998) theology is apparent, as he makes the following observation:

> This, then, is the question: Is a continuous development of the cosmos from its simplest and most original components right up to its present differentiation and complexity, the realm of living being included, acceptable to Christian faith in such a way that it can leave this whole evolution to natural science as a thesis or hypothesis, and then, at most, afterwards include this evolution in a Christian conception of the world? Our answer is yes . . . this sort of general and continuous development implies only that all respective individual realities in their further development possess in the physical and biological realm the characteristic of the possibility of self-transcendence. Each in its own stage can become something else, can change and become "more" ("higher"), whereby this "more" can of course be quite different, cannot, however, be excluded in the development in favor of simply "being different," regardless of whether such a being different would really contain fewer metaphysical questions than a "being more." (p. 38)

Rahner's theological understanding of personhood parallels in certain ways Shanahan's more scientific view, for both are distinctly evolutionary and perhaps even cosmological in character, and therefore in agreement that humanity, life, the world, and matter in general all have a long way to go on the scale of increasing complexity. This is compelling science *and* it is equally compelling theology; taken together, not only dialogically but even more so *integratively*, we are now poised to reflect more in depth on the very real possibility of an unprecedented leap forward for humanity. We become more conscious of our own evolutionary process, we assume a greater role in its development, with the potential for helping to guide it toward loving and wholesome ends, in ways that still reflect the *imago Dei* even if we are technologically enhanced. For example, "intelligence enhancement through nanotechnologies includes realistic possibilities, such as greater and more rapid comprehension, comprehension of what otherwise would be far too complex issues, speeding up and providing solutions for what were once insoluble problems" (Deane-Drummond, 2015, p. 246). In my estimation, this would be something of a positive development, for the global challenges that we are facing seem only to be getting more complex *and* insoluble with each passing day: "climate change, dwindling fossil fuels, ongoing conflicts, widespread poverty, and diseases that remain incurable like cancer and dementia" (Shanahan, 2015, p. 156). Perhaps intelligence and neurocognitive enhancements do not necessarily have to be a violation of the sacred order of things, *if* we can help guide their development in a way that increases the quality and fullness of life for all people. If in fact abundant life or life in all its fullness is the divine intention for all people, as Jesus intimated (John 10:10), then as Karen Lebacqz (2011) suggests, "anything that 'improves' our life and makes it 'fuller' may be countenanced" (p. 58). Furthermore, she adds rhetorically and with technological enhancement in mind, if God is the Creator and we are created *imago Dei*, then, above and beyond merely preserving what is, "are we not also meant to create?" (Lebacqz, 2011, p. 57).

Chapter Four

Maintaining Our Attentional Control

We are nearing a pivotal "tipping point" in human history, if we are not there already, with the steady proliferation of digital technologies and the rapid advance of artificial intelligence. The progress in machine learning has been so swift, largely driven by the advances in deep neural networks and deep learning algorithms, that it has even taken some of the computer science researchers and experts by surprise. Nor can we reverse course and return to a supposed simpler time, a pre-digital age as it were, for even if we could "slow things down" what we have learned is that this would lead to nothing short of an immediate and catastrophic collapse of the national and global economy. As technology continues to permeate every aspect of our lives, it has now become the primary organizing force of the evolutionary process, which means that we are now dependent on it even as we have been and still are dependent on our own human biology. But the day is approaching, perhaps even in a few decades, when we will see biology coalescing with technology, manifested in the merger of humans with machines. I have heard some say that they cannot accept the increasing reach of technology and AI, and therefore have made up their minds to sidestep any technological singularity and biological-technological hybridity. As if it were that simple. While I am all for going off the technology grid as much as possible, even making it a part of my own regular spiritual practice by way of hiking, trekking, contemplative prayer and meditation, and so forth, the reality is that given the ascendance of technology in the evolutionary process, we can no more sidestep or avoid it any more than we could our own biological substratum. As Ilia Delio (2008) has put it so astutely, it is no longer a matter of *dealing with* technology, as if it is something external that we can avoid altogether if we so choose. Rather, technology like biology is now integral to *who we are* as human beings, which will become all the more apparent as we continue to approach the human-machine merger. This is where we as pastoral and spiritual practitioners and those in our care find ourselves at the moment, situated between profound existential opportunity and risk. We still have before us a window of time and opportunity to help guide the process toward just and loving ends, and to help preserve some of the qualities that have made us uniquely human, such as the precious and fragile "gifts" of human consciousness, compassion, and empathy, as long as we can clearly grasp the new terrain that is before us. It will require, individually and collectively, nothing short of the capacity for sustained attention, concentration, and in-depth reflection, something that will not come easy in an ever-accelerating digital world.

PREDISPOSED FOR BREADTH OVER DEPTH

Some of us assume that an increasing amount of time spent on the "screen" compromises our ability to remain focused on a particular issue or task, to maintain, if we put it more technically, our capacity for attentional control. And, there is of course a certain amount of truth to this, even if the only evidence we have to go on is our own personal experience of sitting down at the computer and/or turning on the smartphone. For example, we start out looking for something in particular, but before we know it we are bombarded with breaking political and financial news, algorithmically generated ads that know our preferences and "likes" all too well, and social media updates from friends, family, and colleagues. Moreover, we begin to open this app, and then another and another, and before we know it our original task or issue no longer has our undivided attention but instead now only occupies our attention piecemeal, given the increasing demands in our perceptual field. Notwithstanding the cultural embrace and celebration of multitasking, it is important to know that when it is in the form of "mental juggling" more and more digital information and data, there is a serious downside. In fact, one study (Leiva *et al.*, 2012) has even quantified the "cognitive cost," which happens to be a fourfold increase of time needed to complete the original task, once there is "back and forth switching between applications and unintended interruptions." From a practical standpoint, the finding reveals that if for example my original task is paying bills online, writing an email to a friend, or drafting a report for work that in and of itself would take me about thirty minutes, the fourfold increase of time resulting from attending to so many digital interruptions at once now makes it on average a two-hour project. The switching back and forth between digital apps, ads, updates, text messages, and so forth, while trying to complete the task or find the information that I was working on in the first place, leaves me with a destabilized level of attention and concentration, which along with delaying the completion of the task becomes an impediment to any in-depth reflection about it.

More specifically, there is mounting evidence that frequent use of social media correlates highly with a reduction in attentional control and an increase in attentional distraction for *any* individual, and is in no way limited stereotypically to someone diagnosed with ADHD. In terms of the research, "so far we know that high social media usage is associated with lower levels of attention and self-control," and in fact "people who are more actively engaged in social media also tend to be more easily distracted" (Bermúdez, 2017, pp. 67–68). Earlier we discussed the so-called condition of FOMO (Fear of Missing Out), which seems rampant at the moment due in large measure to all the electronic alerts that we receive by way of our social media apps, such as Facebook, Twitter, Instagram, and Snapchat. If we do not stop what we are doing at least for a moment and immediately check the latest update on breaking news, the uploaded photo of a friend or classmate, and/or a video ad extolling the virtues of the latest cutting-edge product, we might miss out on something important, is what our mind can tell us. But the hijacking of our attention is not merely a matter of the social media alerts and updates themselves, the "external factor," for every time we stop to check on what is trending, what someone we know is doing, and/or what is going on in the world, it triggers an internal reaction, thoughts and feelings about what we are reading or viewing. It is therefore little wonder that people who are more actively engaged in social media become more easily distracted, for the distraction is twofold: (1) a perpetual bombardment of *external* alerts, updates, and messages that we are trying to process, *and* by extension (2) the *internal* thoughts and feelings that are continually triggered by the plethora of information and data. To state the obvious, our psycho-physiological capacities can reach the point of overload if we are not careful, or the point of "saturation" to use Kenneth Gergen's (2000) word. It is the price we pay for living in a rapidly accelerating cyber-world, with our brain and nervous system habituating to the endless digital flow of information and to keeping us on constant alert, so that we do not miss out on anything. "The pace of technology," writes Delio (2013), "is increasing exponentially, outstripping our ability to absorb it or reflect on our use of it" (p. 159).

What we do not know for sure is whether high social media usage is the *cause* of lower levels of attention and self-control, or if the association is simply *correlational*, being one among other contributing factors, along with for example sleep deprivation, poor diet and nutrition, lack of physical activity and exercise, and so on. That said, what we *do* know is that "people who are more actively engaged in social media also tend to be more easily distracted" (Bermúdez, 2017, p. 68), whatever the level of causation. It is best not to get overly hung up on trying to determine what is the root or primary cause of the rise in attentional distraction, the *why* of the problem, but instead to focus more on helping those in our care enhance the capacity for attentional control and stability, cultivating a sense of balance in the midst of all the digital stimuli. It is akin to the general practice of counseling or psychotherapy, where even after getting to the bottom of the origin of the client's psychological problem or disorder, sometimes after months or even years of therapeutic work, she is still at "square one" in a way, needing to reflect on where she goes from here and what she intends to do about it. Therefore, whether or not social media are the primary driving force behind the rise in attentional distraction and instability, we know that there is a correlation between them, which means at the very least that they are "far from being a part of the solution" (Bermúdez, 2017, p. 68). Put another way, "even if social media are not causing this problem, they surely are not helping to solve it" (Bermúdez, 2017, p. 68).

At the same time, as we continue making our way in a digital world with its torrent of data flow, it is necessary that we find ways not only to guide the evolution of technology to just and loving ends, but also more practically to put the resources of social media, the digital apps and assistants, and the algorithmically generated content and information to good use. In becoming metaphoric cyborgs, on our way to a more substantial transformation from biologically-based Homo sapiens to technologically enhanced Techno sapiens, it is imperative that we understand and know how to use twenty-first century technology, otherwise as Harari (2017) noted earlier we risk missing the evolutionary "train" that is about to depart the station, once and for all. It is worth considering that a new form of self-construction and identity is therefore needed in order for us to effectively navigate the digital terrain before us, so that the online self is not necessarily disadvantageous or even undesirable. Indeed, in the context of a digitized world, where technology has fast become the dominant organizing force of the evolutionary process, "the new, online self would thus redefine how we should understand what is truly relevant, making it more about being attuned to the flows of information than about staying focused on my current mission" (Bermúdez, 2017, p. 70). We would, in other words, come to value more highly what is known as attentional breadth, dictated by the rapid and torrential flow of data and information. As Juan Pablo Bermúdez (2017), working in the field of philosophy of mind, has pointed out, the fact is "we may be unable to foresee the new paths of self-construction enabled by the new digital media" (p. 68). Writing in "Social media and self-control: The vices and virtues of attention," his contribution to the important and timely book, *Social media and your brain: Web-based communication is changing how we think and express ourselves*, he adds:

> This may open up new, vast creative spaces that were previously unthinkable, new kinds of activities, skills, and trades. If computers and smartphones are

understood as general-purpose extensions of working memory and the Internet as a general-purpose extension of our senses (both bodily and social), then the possibility exists for novel and unforeseen forms of chunked actions that externalize the cognitive costs onto the computers and the Web, while merging multiple threads of diverse behavioral routines into coherent, basic actions that we have until now been unable to perform. (p. 70)

It might help to know that we are already more neurally predisposed to attentional breadth than attentional depth, the vestiges of an earlier brain that motivated our ancestors to scan as much of the surrounding environment as possible in order to live to see another day. Humans are therefore, by way of evolution, "amazing pattern recognizers, including our ability to see patterns not yet formed," but it comes with a very important caveat: "the cognitive machinery that gives us breadth also limits our ability to concentrate on a single thought deeply through many, many alternatives" (Hendler & Mulvehill, 2016, p. 59). In spending considerable amounts of time on the "screen," whether tracking the latest political or financial updates, checking our social media apps and alerts, and/or invested in a variety of video games simultaneously, we are firing neurons that are connected to attentional breadth, or "multitasking," rather than firing neurons that support the development of attentional stability and sustained concentration. And, the neurons that we fire repeatedly over time on the screen will of course wire together with greater strength and force, into a robust neural circuitry connected to attentional breadth, while that supporting attentional depth and concentration will continue to weaken.

Not that developing a broader and even more accelerated attentional perspective is necessarily a bad thing. For example, studies provide strong evidence that "modern videogames, with their visually rich and fast-paced play, are likely to place significant visuo-spatial and cognitive demands on a gamer, and these demands will in turn leave their mark via the plasticity of their brain and hence on the individual's subsequent behavior—but not necessarily with negative consequences" (Greenfield, 2015, p. 170). It turns out the skills mastered on the screen, in the context of gaming, have the potential for real-world applications: "They include, for example, a superior ability to see small details, faster processing of rapidly presented information, higher capacity in short-term memory, increased capacity to process multiple objects simultaneously, and flexible switching between tasks—all useful skills in a variety of precision-demanding jobs" (Greenfield, 2015, p. 172). We can only wonder if in the future we will look back and conclude that gaming was not as bad as some of us thought it would be, that like so often before throughout human history it was simply a matter of catching up with the times. Looking out over the strange and bewildering digital landscape at present, we could therefore say, in the words of the French anthropologist,

Marc Augé (1995), that we have entered "a world that we have not yet learned to look at" (pp. 35–36), with fewer familiar navigational points to help guide us. Maybe, at least in part, it is simply giving ourselves more time to acclimate to the new terrain:

> A little over a century ago, children were being told to go out and play or help in the garden instead of doing something as unnatural as lying down for hours on end with their nose in a book. Reading was thought to addle their brains, make them weak, and ruin their eyes. As it turned out, reading offered excellent preparation for the dawning information society. Perhaps playing computer games provides a similar grounding for the information intensive and digitalized future that awaits us. (Klingberg, 2009, p. 146)

Still, there is certainly a potential downside, as other studies on video-gaming have determined. Researchers at Iowa State University (Bailey *et al.*, 2010) found that while some video-gaming can improve attention, "high levels of video game experience may be associated with a reduction in the efficiency of processes supporting proactive cognitive control that allow one to maintain goal-directed information processing in contexts that do not naturally hold one's attention." In other words, the gamer has the capacity for more focused attention as long as he or she remains on the screen, immersed in whatever game is occurring. Off the screen, however, is a much different story as the study reveals, in the context of more ordinary living and commonplace routine. "Or to put it more simply," writes Susan Greenfield (2015), commenting on the Iowa State study, "gaming could be bad for sustained attention," for what it reveals is that "videogames may train an individual to respond rapidly to suddenly presented stimuli, but they may provide no advantage in being able to maintain focus during mundane tasks" (p. 175). A potential "cognitive cost," then, for the average gamer is that real-world living will not capture and sustain his or her attention in the same way that virtual reality can, for it cannot begin to provide the same consistent dopamine rush that is now needed to activate the attentional circuitry. While there can be cognitive benefits to spending substantial amounts of time on the screen, namely developing useful skills applicable to certain real-world situations and precision-demanding jobs, the problem is that this misses the overall bigger picture of how humans in general develop skills and competencies. "It loses sight of one key feature of skill acquisition: it is slow, it is hard, it is effortful, and it requires persistence" (Bermúdez, 2017, p. 71), which presupposes more focused and sustained attention over time.

Even after reaching an advanced level of skill, whether as an athlete, artist, musician, and so forth, "in order for experts to perform at their best, they need to stay focused," and this "implies great endogenous control of attention" (Bermúdez, 2017, p. 71). Put in the language of Eastern spiritual traditions, it implies learning to cultivate one-pointed or single-pointed concentration, in order to develop more fully the particular skill or competency that is needed to flourish individually and collectively. At the moment and for the foreseeable future, the culture will not even remotely be in support of our cultivating any sustained attention, but rather driven by the proliferation and accelerated advance of digital technologies, will actually be working against it. "Acquiring a skill in more distracting environments requires even more endogenous control, because agents need control over their attention to thread the multiple behavioral components into a meaningful unified action" (Bermúdez, 2017, p. 71). In the long run the human brain will ultimately find a way to adapt to any environment, even the accelerated digital world, as it has done down through the course of human history, for as we noted in the last chapter it is a most remarkable adaptation machine. Only now it must keep up with the unprecedented rate of evolutionary change, with technology increasingly in the driver's seat, so that in a way we can expect our brain almost out of necessity to be working against the acquisition of sustained attention and concentration, as well as against the "skill" of contemplative reflection. And, without the foundation of attentional stability and sustained reflection, particularly in the context of ordinary living and mundane circumstances, it is difficult to imagine preserving and cultivating over time the most precious and fragile of human skills and virtues, including our compassion, empathy, and consciousness-based creativity. Without an enhanced level of attentional control in today's digital world, "what is most likely," writes Bermúdez (2017), "is that in the short run, agents end up lost in their multitasking, having forgotten mid-performance what it was they were trying to do in the first place; and in the long run, agents will end up unable to create new, flourishing skills and virtuous selves, rather generating incoherent, haphazard characters and identities" (p. 71).

To be sure, this is a worrisome development, precisely at a time when there is so much at stake for the world, the planet, the human individual and the collective human race. Our digital culture demands that we move with it commensurately, at an ever-accelerating rate and therefore with little time for a moment's pause to concentrate and deeply reflect on the pressing issues before us. Before long the brain, yours and mine, learns to adapt to the new terrain, because this is what it does, preoccupied with our survival. As we noted earlier, with the world changing in dramatic and unprecedented ways, the human brain is changing with it in equally unprecedented ways, until it establishes a new baseline or a "new normal" for life in a digital world. The emerging new normal, however, as Bermúdez (2017) notes, has an obvious downside, for "the rise of immediate, massive, interactive media has coincided with the rise of an emotivism and intuition in the public sphere that tends to bury dispassionate reflection and reasoned debate under a mountain of gut feelings and intense reactions, all quickly expressed, replicated, and made viral through Facebook and Twitter" (p. 72). And, once again, it is happening at a time when there is so much at stake for human beings and the entire planet, with biological life approaching a pivotal tipping point. We are facing climate change on a global scale, dwindling fossil fuels, biological annihilation, human overpopulation and overconsumption, widespread poverty and economic inequality, tribalism and incivility, all of which require our most undivided attention and thoughtful reflection *if* we intend to help guide the evolutionary process toward more hopeful ends. Yet all too often any hint of deeper reflection is drowned out by the crescendo of tweets and sound bites, the "new normal" form of social discourse for a digital culture. "So what we might ultimately be losing," adds Bermúdez (2017), "is the very possibility of a functional, reflective democracy that is capable of discussing a topic without being distracted away from the topic by a tweetworthy, rhetorical sleight of hand" (p. 72). Interestingly, the possibility exists that digital technologies and machine intelligence could help us discern a way forward, if we can find ways to put them to good use toward benevolent and compassionate ends. The problem, as we learned earlier, is more human than anything else, whether technology will ultimately become more existential opportunity than risk, or the other way around. At the moment, it would seem that our use of technology, particularly when it comes to social media, seems to be pulling more in the direction of existential risk, "favoring attentional breadth over attentional depth, brief spouts of impulse over careful and dispassionate reflection" (Bermúdez, 2017, p. 72).

AN EXTRAORDINARY ADAPTATION MACHINE

The human brain is an adaptation and survival machine par excellence, so as it has been doing throughout human history, we can fully expect it to continue adapting to the present and future landscape. Only now, as it habituates to the unprecedented world of digital technologies and machine intelligence, its powers of adaptation will be tested like never before, and in so many ways pushed to the limits. Given the exponential increase of the digital universe and with it machine-generated data, in no time at all when viewed evolutionarily, "it is hard to understand," writes Greenfield (2015), "how the human brain will absorb such a tsunami of information" (p. 254). We can expect it to focus first and foremost on our survival, seeing us through the digital revolution that is already well underway, even if it means our transitioning from Homo to Techno sapiens. As far as the brain is concerned, in particular the parts of the brain that are older and therefore more primordial, including the brainstem and directly above it the limbic system, it makes little difference if we remain purely biological beings or if we become more enhanced humans reflecting a biological-technological hybridity: as long as we can survive, in some shape or form. Whether that eventual shape and form is still inclusive of the qualities that have made us uniquely human for millennia, those that have been necessary for human development and flourishing to occur, such as consciousness, compassion, empathy, is less of an overall concern to the brain when it is in a heightened state of survival mode. And this is where it will be for the foreseeable future, doing its best to absorb let alone process and meaningfully reflect on the tsunami of machine-generated data and information coming its way, day after day, minute by minute. Nor can we assume the digital "storm" to abate anytime soon, if ever, which could leave us feeling as if we are frequently near if not beyond the point of saturation. "Technology pushes us along at such rapid speeds that the human brain cannot absorb the information sufficiently to process. Hence, we are increasingly overwhelmed and fragmented" (Delio, 2013, p. 166).

What we do know for sure at this pivotal and unprecedented time in human history, and in brain evolution, is that our neural pathways are being rerouted at a speed like never before, as the brain attempts to keep up with the digital revolution. Continual exposure to the "screen," and with it the torrent of digital information, whether by way of smartphones, computers, video games, search engines, and/or social media, "stimulates brain cell alteration and neurotransmitter release, gradually strengthening new neural pathways in our brains while weakening old ones" (Small & Vorgan, 2008, p. 1). The fundamental issue, of course, as we continue moving toward the technological singularity and with it the increasing merger of machine and human intelligence, is being very clear about the pathways that are in fact weakening: those connected with sustained attention that support a social and relational way of living. "As the brain evolves and shifts its focus toward new technological skills, it drifts away from fundamental social skills, such as reading facial expressions during conversation or grasping the emotional context of a subtle gesture" (Small & Vorgan, 2008, p. 2). Before we witness a full-scale intelligence explosion, with the advent of artificial general (human-level) intelligence (AGI) and perhaps shortly thereafter the emergence of artificial superintelligence (ASI), we must ask ourselves: do we want to hold on to our "fundamental social skills," along with other fragile and precious qualities that have made us human for so long? If so, then we must be very intentional about preserving and enhancing the capacity for attentional control and sustained reflection, while there is still a window of time and opportunity, for the brain on autopilot in a digital world will be much more focused on helping us rapidly develop and build up skills that enable technological enhancement.

It is extraordinary to remember that this dramatic leap in human brain development, occurring in the midst of the digital revolution, "has rapidly emerged over a single generation and may represent one of the most unexpected yet pivotal advances in human history" (Small & Vorgan, 2008, p. 2). What it reflects is the epistemological framework and taken-for-granted ways of knowing of younger minds, so-called "digital natives" who, as we have noted, know no other way of life other than the culture of the "screen," unlike "digital immigrants" who began adapting to it later in life, well beyond their formative years. It is, so to speak, the "air" that young adults and those younger breathe *and* have been breathing for as long as they can remember, which takes the idea of a "generation gap" to a whole new level. In his research, Gary Small (Small & Vorgan, 2008) has found that "as a consequence of this overwhelming and early high-tech stimulation of the digital native's brain, we are witnessing the beginning of a deeply divided *brain gap* between younger and older minds—in just *one* generation:"

> What used to be simply a *generation gap* that separated young people's values, music, and habits from those of their parents has now become a huge divide resulting in two separate cultures. The brains of the younger generation are digitally hardwired from toddlerhood, often at the expense of neural circuitry that controls one-on-one people skills. Individuals of the older generation face a world in which their brains *must* adapt to high technology, or they will be left behind—politically, socially, and economically. . . . During this pivotal point in brain evolution, natives and immigrants alike can learn the tools they need to take charge of their lives and brains, while both preserving their humanity and keeping up with the latest technology. We do not all have to become techno-zombies, nor do we need to trash our computers and go back to writing longhand. Instead, we all should help our brains adapt and succeed in this ever-accelerating technological environment. (pp. 3–4)

There is strong indication that the brain has already been adapting to the revolutionary world of high technology, well before any merger of human and machine intelligence. In attending to the perpetual flow of digital information, we are strengthening, as we learned earlier, cognitive abilities *and* forms of attention associated with enhanced visuo-spatial coordination, faster problem-solving and processing of rapidly presented information, an increased capacity to process multiple objects at the same time, and flexible switching between tasks. In order to cope with the digital torrent, "we develop a better ability to sift through large amounts of information rapidly and decide what is important and what is not—our mental filters basically learn how to shift into overdrive" (Small & Vorgan, 2008, p. 21). And, this is only the beginning of the shift into overdrive for our cognitive filters, with the brain, increasingly more technologically enhanced, achieving far greater levels of digital adaptation. "Rather than simply catching 'digital ADD,' many of us are developing neural circuitry that is customized for rapid and incisive spurts of directed concentration" (Small & Vorgan, 2008, p. 21). So, we seem to be developing attentional control after all, specifically in ways that we as technologically enhanced human beings will surely need both in the short and particularly in the longer term, if we ever hope to survive and flourish in the digital world. Still, it is important to note that the enhanced neural circuitry involved is connected primarily to cognitive functioning, so that not surprisingly we are seeing a rise in average IQ scores simultaneous with the digital revolution. As Small (Small & Vorgan, 2008) notes, "although the digital evolution of our brains increases social isolation and diminishes the spontaneity of interpersonal relationships, it may well be increasing our intelligence in the way we currently measure and define IQ" (p. 21).

This is all well and good in terms of enhancing our cognitive abilities and potential, but it does raise a rather obvious and sobering question: what about the simultaneous "drift away" from other abilities and qualities, such as social and relational skills that have long been fundamental to human identity? Are we, and in particular digital natives in a transitional phase, on the cusp of leaving behind certain abilities that once basic to our individual and collective survival have less evolutionary significance in a digital world? Digital natives and more than a few digital immigrants, for example, now pursue intimate and romantic relationships mostly by way of online dating, "with couples preferring to get to know each other first through the distance and safety of their smartphones" (Greenfield, 2015, p. 131). This is far from a minor or inconsequential detail, for what it reveals is that technology skills are fast becoming sequentially primary in the area of human relations, romantic or otherwise, whereas social and relational skills are increasingly more secondary, something that we can get to eventually in becoming couples or friends. On the one hand, it certainly goes with the territory, given the digital revolution and proliferation of social media, yet on the other hand it raises some serious concerns if we are hoping to help guide the evolutionary process, our own evolution toward loving, compassionate, empathic ends. For these are fundamentally social and relational skills, and as such they require something additional to cognitive intelligence, something above and beyond mere IQ. If we put it in the language of Daniel Goleman (2005), love, compassion, and empathy tap into neural circuitry connected to EQ, emotional intelligence, which in turn supports the fostering of social and relational intelligence. But, this is the very neural circuitry that at present is weakening, as more and more the brain, moving into overdrive, shifts its focus to developing and building up new technological skills.

Earlier, Nicholas Carr (2010) pointed out that given the plasticity of the brain, we can be certain that our online habits continue to reverberate in our neural pathways and synapses, even when we are not online. As we devote considerable time and attention to life on the screen, the "new normal" baseline, we are in fact strengthening certain cognitive skills and corresponding neural circuitry associated with increased IQ, for example "our ability to speedily evaluate objects and other stimuli as they appear in the abstract realm of a computer screen" (Carr, 2010, p. 148). But, argues Carr (2010), a faster and more cognitively efficient brain does not necessarily mean that it is "better;" rather, "it just means that we have different brains" (p. 148). Part of the existential risk in becoming at the very least more technologically enhanced human beings, if not on our way to becoming Techno sapiens, is that our "EQ," our capacity for emotional as well as social and relational intelligence, is not increasing with our IQ. In fact, it might be heading in the opposite direction, as the neural processes supporting it become less active, given our attachment to the screen. Our higher emotions, such as compassion and empathy, emerge from neural circuitry and pathways that do not operate in rapid-fire overdrive, but instead develop more gradually over time.

Antonio Damasio's research team (Immordino-Yang *et al.*, 2009), at the Brain and Creativity Institute at USC, have found in a landmark study that in order to feel compassionate and empathic about the psychological situation of another human being, additional time is needed for what they call "introspective processing." But, "the rapidity and parallel processing of attention-requiring information, which hallmark the digital age, might reduce the frequency of full experience of such emotions, with potentially negative consequences" (Immordino-Yang *et al.*, 2009). Carr (2010), in commenting on the Damasio team's research findings, adds:

> It is not only deep thinking that requires a calm, attentive mind. It is also empathy and compassion . . . Damasio and his colleagues had subjects listen to stories describing people experiencing physical or psychological pain. The subjects were then put into a magnetic resonance imaging machine and their brains were scanned as they were asked to remember the stories. The experiment revealed that while the human brain reacts very quickly to demonstrations of physical pain—when you see someone injured, the primitive pain centers in your own brain activate almost instantaneously—the more sophisticated mental processes of empathizing with psychological suffering unfolds much more slowly. . . . The experiment, say the scholars, indicates that the more distracted we become, the less able we are to experience the subtlest, most distinctively human forms of empathy, compassion, and other emotions. (p. 220–221)

The subtlest and most distinctive forms of human emotion are nothing short of miraculous when considered within the vastness of cosmic time and space. As Steven Pinker has already said of consciousness, and the same would apply to the high emotions of empathy and compassion, nothing gives life more purpose than the realization that every moment of consciousness, every moment of introspective processing of the psychological situation of another human being, is a most precious and fragile "gift." The miracle, as we discussed in the previous chapter, is not that consciousness and our higher emotions, as they are presently constituted, suddenly appeared out of nowhere, but rather that their emergence has been a far more complex, circuitous, and protracted evolutionary process. These subtle and fragile gifts are therefore something to be preserved and nurtured in the midst of a digital age, while we still have a window of time and opportunity, before machine learning achieves and eventually surpasses human-level intelligence. But they will not be preserved *unless* we can find ways to periodically and very intentionally "slow down" in this rapid-fire digital world, to live more contemplatively, which presupposes that we are reinforcing and strengthening our capacity for attentional control, in-depth reflection, and introspective processing. Carr (2010) writes that while "it would be rash to jump to the conclusion that the Internet is undermining our moral sense," it is not at all rash to suggest that "as the Net reroutes our vital paths and diminishes our capacity for contemplation, it is altering the depth of our emotions as well as our thoughts" (p. 221). Which is to say that it is altering the very fabric of human consciousness and human nature, not only what we think and feel but even more profoundly *who we are* as human beings. If we are not taking care in our lives and in our work to preserve and nurture the fundamental capacity for sustained attention and concentration, then "the tumultuous advance of technology could, like the arrival of the locomotive at the Concord station, drown out the refined perceptions, thoughts, and emotions that arise only through contemplation and reflection" (Carr, 2010, p. 222). The brain, as it has been doing all along, will inevitably adapt to its surroundings and in this case to life on the screen, if it has not done so already, but not without a potential cost: the weakening of our capacity for attentional control. "Thanks once again to the plasticity of our neuronal pathways, the more we use the Web, the more we train our brain to be distracted—to process information very quickly and very efficiently but without sustained attention" (Carr, 2010, p. 194).

HOLDING ON TO OUR HUMANITY

Whether the technological singularity and the fuller merger of human intelligence with machines occurs in the middle or latter part of this century, or not until next century, it is remarkable to think that digital immigrants, those of us who were not born into the digital world but rather came upon it later in life, will be the last generation to remember firsthand what life and the world were like before there was an Internet and Web. With technology becoming increasingly more powerful and central to the whole evolutionary process, it is clear that we are now beyond the point of no return. At the same time, perhaps there is something that digital immigrants can pass on to future generations of digital natives, while there is still a window of time and opportunity, something that for millennia has been unique and precious to human experience, such as the capacity for in-depth introspective processing and reflection. It does assume, however, that even in the midst of the digital torrent, we are able to maintain attentional control long enough to take, if we put it spiritually, a "sacred pause." The writer, Michael Harris (2014), offers a rather profound meditation on this rare and pivotal moment in human history, and it is worth quoting at length:

> Soon enough, nobody will remember life before the Internet. What does this unavoidable fact mean? For those billions who come next, of course, it will not mean anything very obvious. Our online technologies, taken as a whole, will have become a kind of foundational myth—a story people are barely conscious of, something natural and, therefore, unnoticed. . . . We have in this brief historical moment, this moment in between two modes of being, a very rare opportunity. For those of us who have lived both with and without the vast, crowded connectivity the Internet provides, these are the few days when we can still notice the differences between Before and After. This is the moment. Our awareness of this singular position pops up every now and again. We catch ourselves idly reaching for our phones at the bus stop. Or we notice how, mid-conversation, a fumbling friend dives into the perfect recall of Google. We can still catch ourselves. We say, Wait. I think that within the mess of changes we are experiencing, there is a single difference that we feel most keenly; and it is also the difference that future generations will find hardest to grasp. That is the end of absence—the loss of lack. The daydreaming silences in our lives are filled; the burning solitudes are extinguished. Before all memory of these absences is shuttered, though, there is this brief time when we might record what came before. We might do something with those small, barely noticeable instances when we are reminded of our love for absence. They flash at us amid the rush of our experience and seem to signal: Wait, wasn't there something . . .? (pp. 7–8).

This is a rare and precious moment, an eschatological moment if we look at it theologically, as we transition from human life as we have known it as Homo sapiens into uncharted territory. Already we are technologically enhanced humans, and perhaps before too long we will take an even more dramatic evolutionary leap, becoming Techno sapiens. We will not have a moment like this again to reflect on who we have been, who we want to become in a digital world, how we intend to help guide the process toward loving and compassionate ends, and how we will avoid completely losing our humanity given the accelerated advance of machine intelligence. Precisely because we have this moment to reflect on how we want to help guide the process, because we still have some choice regarding our use of digital technologies and artificial intelligence, "we had better," writes Harari (2017), "understand what is happening and make up our minds about it before it makes up our minds for us" (p. 55). Indeed, as we have seen, AI is increasingly making up our minds for us, and yet there is still a moment for us to say, "Wait," and not let the window of opportunity pass us by. What we need to make up our minds about, sooner rather than later, is what we want to preserve of our humanity in a world that is and will continue to be dominated by machine intelligence. Bostrom (2016) refers to it as "crunch time," as "we find ourselves in a thicket of strategic complexity, surrounded by a dense mist of uncertainty" (p. 314). But we cannot sit idly by, hoping and praying that somehow things will work out for the best, or that God will miraculously intervene just in the nick of time to stem the exponential growth of AI, keeping us from becoming a more complete biological-technological hybridity. Even if the intelligence explosion occurs decades from now, the challenge we face at present is "to hold on to our humanity: to maintain our groundedness, common sense, and good-humored decency even in the teeth of this most unnatural and inhuman problem" (Bostrom, 2016, p. 320). Moreover, holding on to our humanity means, as we have been discussing, the preservation of our capacity for sustained attention and introspective reflection, without which "good-humored decency" and human compassion and empathy will be in short supply. "We need to bring," argues Bostrom (2016), "all our human resourcefulness to bear on its solution," for holding on to our humanity in a digital world is now "the essential task of our age" (p. 320).

It is telling that even in the world of wearable technology and electronics, where business as you might expect is booming, we are being encouraged not to lose sight of our humanity even as we are offered an overabundance of digital products. For example, in an article (Sharia, 2015) reporting on the development of "futuristic baby monitors," there is now a "wearable onesie" and a "smart baby bootie" designed to keep us up-to-date about the vital signs of our babies, by constantly transmitting the data to the parent's smartphone. The article, written for the newsletter of Wearables.com, ends by reminding technologically sophisticated parents of "One more thing: Don't forget to be a human." Even coming from the world of technology itself, we are at times reminded not to lose our humanity, in this case not to completely turn over control of parenting our young children to omnipresent digital assistants and convenient baby-monitor apps. If we do not take great care to grasp and understand what is happening to the world and to us in the midst of this momentous digital revolution, to make up our minds about how we want to live as humans even as we go about putting to good use the digital technologies, then as Harari (2017) makes clear the AI-based technologies will be moving exceedingly fast to make up our minds for us. And, this pivotal and precious historical moment, this rare moment of opportunity to hold on to what is most distinct and even good about our humanity, our social and relational skills, our emotional intelligence, our good-humored decency, our compassion and empathy, will have come and gone. "All of us," writes Gary Small (2008), "digital natives and immigrants, will master new technologies and take advantage of their efficiencies, but we also need to maintain our people skills and humanity" (p. 22). It is, to be sure, this careful balancing act between learning to master and put to good use the digital technologies and at the same time preserving what makes us unique as human beings, the essential and urgent task of our age.

And yet, as we have discussed, studies are already revealing that as we continue to adapt to the world of digital technologies and to life on the perpetual screen, we are giving far less attention to "people skills" than we used to. For example, our aptitude for reading facial expressions, for grasping the emotional context of subtle gestures, and for interpreting the nuances of human communication, verbal and non-verbal, is weakening. And, if this is only the beginning of the digital revolution, with the emergence of artificial narrow intelligence (ANI), we can only wonder how much or perhaps how little attention we will be giving to maintaining people skills once artificial general or human-level intelligence (AGI) is upon us. Even now, "with the weakening of the brain's neural circuitry controlling human contact, our social interactions may become awkward, and we tend to misinterpret, and even miss subtle, nonverbal messages" (Small and Vorgan, 2008, p. 2). This is no small matter, particularly at a time of heightened tension and mistrust for our nation and world, when there is an upsurge of nuclear saber-rattling. "Imagine how the continued slipping of social skills might affect an international summit meeting . . . when a misread facial cue or a misunderstood gesture could make the difference between escalating military conflict or peace" (Small and Vorgan, 2008, p. 2). Even in the lives of ordinary human beings, who are not involved in international summits or nuclear peace talks, imagine how the weakening of neural circuitry connected to interpersonal interactions will affect everyday life and discourse in homes, classrooms, and work settings, how it is already affecting it. The social and relational cost for individuals, families, schools, businesses, and faith communities is potentially great if we are not giving an equal share of attention to being human, to enhancing our people skills even as we master the new digital technologies.

Earlier in this chapter we noted that there is a correlation between high usage of social media and lower levels of sustained attention and self-control, the latter being necessary and even fundamental to the development of effective people skills. Moreover, we learned of a study quantifying the "cognitive cost" of frequent back and forth switching between all of the digital interruptions, the alerts, ads, and messages: a fourfold increase of time needed to complete an original task. Trying to complete the original task while mentally juggling more and more digital information at the same time leaves us with a destabilized level of attention and a diminished capacity for any indepth reflection. But what if the original task is something other than, for example, writing a report for work on the computer, paying bills online, or researching travel web sites for vacation ideas? What if it was something more *relational*, a difficult or even painful matter that a friend, a loved one, a colleague has brought to our attention, either in person or online, hoping for a timely and compassionate response? It is one thing to calculate the *cognitive* cost of attending to and then switching back and forth between all the digital interruptions, as we are trying to complete an original task, which on average will take us four times as long to get it done. Depending on how often we let ourselves get digitally distracted during the day, while trying to focus on other matters at hand, it could very well be a substantial cognitive cost in terms of increased attentional distraction, not to mention precious time and productivity that is wasted. But what about the *relational* cost of getting digitally distracted, of switching back and forth between the alerts from the world of politics, finance, entertainment, and sports, between the algorithmically generated pop-up ads, and between the social-media updates and messages at the same time a friend or loved one needs our undivided attention and thoughtful feedback? Is it even possible to calculate or quantify the relational and emotional cost stemming from FOMO-driven distraction, of being increasingly less attentive to and present with those in our lives? It may in fact be incalculable, for what is at stake is our humanity, what has made us uniquely human for so long, including our cognitive intelligence or IQ, but also our emotional and relational intelligence, our people skills.

"The ability to care about and share others' emotional experiences is something that clearly differentiates humans from most of the rest of the animal kingdom" (Greenfield, 2015, p. 133), and is therefore worth preserving as we move further into the digital revolution. At the same time, there is evidence from studies to suggest that our ability to be empathic is in steady decline. Greenfield (2015) notes an important meta-analysis of fourteen thousand U.S. college students spanning more than thirty years, which revealed that overall levels of empathy have been in decline, with a steeper drop in the more recent years of the study—"a time frame that corresponds well with the advent of social networking among digital natives" (p. 36). The authors (Konrath *et al.*, 2011) of the study, commenting on their own findings, also call our attention to the more recent time frame and similarly "the meteoric rise in popularity of social networking sites . . . as younger people more frequently remove themselves from deep interpersonal social situations and become immersed in isolated online environments." Whether social media are the primary driving force behind the decline in empathy, the cause as it were, or as we discussed earlier if the association is more correlational, in either case we know that even if they are not causing the reduction in attentional control and the decline in empathy, social media are certainly not helping to solve the problem. "These physically distant online environments," the authors (Konrath *et al.*, 2011) of the meta-analysis observe, "could functionally create a buffer between individuals, which makes it easier to ignore others' pain or even at times inflict pain on others." To the meteoric rise in social networking sites, we could also add within the same recent time frame the sharp rise in the rate of cyberbullying. It is quite disturbing to learn that more than a third of adolescents in general report having been cyberbullied, with the rate even higher for adolescent girls (Cyberbullying Research Center, 2016). Perhaps it is more than coincidental that a decline in social empathy is simultaneous with an increase in online relationships: "If you hurt someone's feelings but cannot see the other person's reaction, you will lack sufficient cues to understand what you have done and apologize or take some other compensatory action" (Greenfield, 2015, p. 134). Put in the 12-Step language of Alcoholics Anonymous (AA), in not knowing or understanding the full extent of what we have done to another person, how we have inflicted pain, we cannot make "direct amends" (Step 9). "The increase in feelings of isolation may be connected with the ease and speed with which personal information can be posted, which may encourage people to thoughtlessly send potentially damaging information out into the world" (Greenfield, 2015, p. 134–135).

It is important to remember that neuroplasticity, the brain's remarkable capacity to change its own functioning, can work either way, in the interest of human growth and development and in the other direction, toward reinforcing the most primitive and aggressive instincts of our human nature. It all depends on what neural circuitry we are firing the most, in our personal lives and collectively as a society. The human brain, as it has done from the very beginning, will learn to adapt to its surroundings, one way or another, whether the environment be hunter-gatherer, agricultural, industrial, or at present digital. The only difference is that the digital environment, the world of machine intelligence, is a world unlike any before, so that in terms of how the brain will ultimately adapt to it, only time will tell. At present, it is trying to handle the tsunami of digital information coming its way at seeming light speed, an unprecedented historical development to be sure, and to think that it is only the beginning of what is to come, when mere "rudimentary" artificial narrow intelligence (ANI) gives way to a more highly advanced artificial general intelligence (AGI), and perhaps not long after to artificial superintelligence (ASI). How will we ever hold on to our humanity then, our capacity for attentional control, introspective reflection, compassion and empathy, and good-humored decency? For the time being at least, we still have a window, a moment of opportunity to preserve and foster these unique and precious qualities that have made us uniquely human, before the moment is gone. The implications for pastoral and spiritual practitioners working with individuals, couples, families, and faith communities, all trying to find their way in a digital world, are profound and will become more obvious in the remaining chapters. For, as Nick Bostrom (2016) has argued, this is the essential task of our time, to hold on to our humanity, and must therefore become a central focus of our work in a digital world.

Chapter Five

Elevating Contemplative-Meditational Practice

In recent years, I have heard congregants, clergy, and denominational leaders at times lamenting the steady decline of church membership, noting in particular the glaring absence of youth and young adults from the pews, the digital natives. Whether the lament is expressed at a church council meeting, a gathering of regional or national judicatory representatives, during an adult education class, and/or from the pulpit, it is often in the form of, "Where have all the young people gone?" Indeed, an increasingly common trend in local congregations is for children to grow up in the church, be confirmed as members when reaching adolescence, and then rarely to be seen again. Some of us may assume that this simply reflects a developmental moratorium, in which "adolescents become more distant to, or even leave the church, but that they will be ready to come back in adulthood. The moratorium is not permanent" (Schweitzer, 2004, p. 70). It may last for a few years, perhaps a decade or more, this phase of distancing or even "rebellion," but the hope is that given enough time, young people who have left the church in their adolescent years will eventually "show the same degree of religious affiliation as their parents' generation does" (Schweitzer, 2004, p. 70). No need to get alarmed, in other words, it is simply a matter of waiting for young people to grow up and assume their rightful place in society and within social institutions, even if in a digital world the process of maturation is taking a bit longer. But, as Friedrich Schweitzer (2004) has argued, this may be little more than wishful thinking, the inevitability that somehow, someway we can "bring today's young people back to the church in the future" (p. 70). As we are learning from recent landmark demographic studies (Pew Research Center, 2015), America's religious landscape is changing dramatically, with more and more millennials, i.e., digital natives, leaving organized religion with no intention of ever returning. Therefore, when it comes to Generation Y, the millennials, let alone Generation Z, the post-millennials, it is probably best not to get our hopes up for an inevitable return to the church.

A MYSTIC OR NOTHING AT ALL

How do we account for a precipitous decline in religious affiliation among millennials? Sometimes I hear technology getting the blame, that religion in general and the church in particular simply cannot compete with all the digital offerings readily available by way of a smartphone. There is certainly some truth to this common assumption, for as we have seen, technology and machine intelligence is now a formidable force in human life, clearly impacting in profound and unprecedented ways the lives of all of us, digital natives as well as digital immigrants. The only difference, and it is a significant difference to be sure, is that digital natives were *born into* and as a result have lived their *formative* developmental years in the world of digital technologies, almost as if they and the technologies have been growing up together, side by side. Other times, I hear it said that the absence of younger people in religious settings is proof that they are not as spiritual as older generations, that they are more self-centered and less concerned about sacred matters and issues. It is important to understand that demographic studies and research do *not* support the latter assumption that millennials are any less spiritual; rather, they simply have other ways of expressing it than those prescribed by organized religion. For example, as millennials are keenly aware that the world they are inheriting is nearing a pivotal tipping point, their "religion" is increasingly invested in matters that are unambiguously *spiritual,* such as environmental sustainability, gender and racial equality, economic justice, *and* finding inner peace and balance in these anxious and uncertain times. It is therefore not surprising that another Pew Research study (Pew Research Center, 2014) has found that the frequency of meditational practice with millennials is steadily rising. Having personally attended a recent mindfulness-meditation retreat in upstate New York, I was struck firsthand by the overflow turnout of youth and young-adult women and men, and recall saying to myself throughout the weekend, "So, this is where the young people have gone!"

Perhaps there is something reciprocal that digital natives can pass on to digital immigrants, in the form of a spirituality that is grounded, not exclusively in a system of codified religious belief and doctrine, but in contemplative-meditational *practice.* The generation that has never known a world without the Internet, and with it the perpetual flow of digital information, continues gravitating toward mindfulness meditational practices, even as it moves away from the world of organized religion. Maybe there is something that digital natives intuitively grasp far better than digital immigrants, that in order to find even a modicum of inner calm and balance in the midst of the unrelenting digital torrent, one will need not only a framework of "right belief" but also spiritual *practices* that explicitly foster attentional control and sustained concentration. It is important to point out that there is a growing body of neuroscientific research confirming this "intuitive understanding," that the stabilization of attention, foundational to inner *and* relational well-being, can be supported *and* strengthened over time through a regular contemplative practice. I will have more to say about the science later, specifically the findings of contemplative neuroscientific research. For now, it is worth noting that Karl Rahner (1971), displaying an uncanny prescience or, in keeping with his theology of *Vorgriff*, a remarkable pre-apprehension of what was soon to come, once said famously, "The Christian of the future will either be a 'mystic,' one who has 'experienced' something, or will cease to be anything at all" (p. 15). It is almost as if he had the present digital age in mind, and digital natives in particular, who with increasing frequency are embracing a "quasi-mystical religion" in the form of contemplative-meditational practice, or they will have no religion at all.

Religion and spirituality is of course, for the literal mystic and maybe even for the digital-native "mystic" as well, a matter of directly experiencing the divine or the ground of being. It is therefore more contemplative and less conceptual in nature, less mediated by systems of religious belief and elaborate theological construction. Rahner (1971) would certainly not be advocating doing away with religious beliefs and doctrine, nor with core teachings of the church, and yet at the same time his prescient statement clearly conveys something of a warning for religious faith communities, now situated in a very different digital world. In coming years, digital natives, whether they be millennials or the post-millennial generation that follows, will be embracing a more "mystical" form of religion, or more precisely a more contemplative-meditational approach to spirituality, in order to find and maintain a sense of balance and equilibrium. This trend of "being a mystic or nothing at all," in other words, will not be temporary, but rather is fast becoming a permanent reality, necessitated by the rapid advance of technology. Indeed, how can the digital native, or even the digital immigrant for that matter, how can anyone maintain any sense of psychological balance and equilibrium in today's cyberworld without having a spiritual practice that keeps us directly and experientially centered in divine presence and energy? In general, digital natives are focused on spiritual practices that will help them find an inner sense of calm and peace, and will also provide a direct encounter with and experience of the divine, whether the experience is mediated by a religious belief system or not. It must be understood, then, that the pursuit of a more direct and immediate experience of God goes with the territory for many digital natives, as immediacy after all is their epistemological way of knowing, a reflection of growing up in the world of digital technologies.

This is not at all meant to downplay the modus operandi of digital natives, for once again I would argue that there is something reciprocal that they can teach and pass on to older generations of digital immigrants in the form of, with Rahner (1971) in mind, a more "mystical" spirituality grounded in contemplative-meditational *practice*. It is worth noting that for Rahner (1978) a pre-apprehension of infinite being or of God is ultimately beyond any conceptual system of belief, beyond our religious or theological knowledge, and comes by way of a direct and contemplative experience of divine presence. To be clear, this does *not* imply that a religious belief system and theological framework is unimportant, for even if it must be distinguished from a direct experience of the divine, "the conceptualization does play a significant role in *shaping* the experience" (Kilby, 2004, p. 21). Still, the direct contemplative experience of God is primary for Rahner (1971), so much so that in the days ahead, *these* days of digital living, the digital native will either be a "mystic," experiencing God or infinite being firsthand, or nothing at all. Karen Kilby (2004), writing in *Karl Rahner: Theology and Philosophy*, puts it this way:

> It is necessary to distinguish, Rahner insists again and again, between an *original* level of knowledge, or experience, or existence, and the level on which we use words and concepts. We use concepts to verbalize, thematize, or objectify our original experience, but the latter is never fully captured, never exhausted, by these concepts. The original experience always remains richer than any articulation of it, always eludes a complete verbalization. . . . The pre-apprehension of being, then, is pre-thematic, and is not to be confused with any concepts with which it may be described. As distinct from other things that might also be called pre-thematic, however, (such as moods and emotions), it is *also* to be distinguished from concepts in that it is the condition of the possibility of *every* concept, even those which may be used to describe it. (p. 21)

There are parallels between Rahner's emphasis on a contemplative pre-apprehension of being and of God, and what the Zen practitioner would call a "direct knowing," a direct and ultimately unmediated encounter with infinite being and with the fullness of human life and experience. In either case, it is the quintessential form of human spirituality, a deeply embodied and integrated spiritual experience that is not reduced primarily to a cognitive knowing, simply to a conceptual and intellectual grasp of religious tenets and theological precepts. And, it is ours to still preserve and cultivate in this window of time and opportunity, *before* we are in the midst of an even greater intelligence explosion, with the arrival of human-level machine learning. Perhaps the earlier discussion of holding on to our humanity and preserving the fundamental qualities that have made us uniquely human for millennia can be distilled down to what we are describing now, namely the preservation of human spirituality as we have known it. Before long, the brain, in the interest of our evolution if not survival, will be pushing us to keep up with a far more accelerated digital world, and we will have less time to focus and reflect on what it is about our humanity that we most want to preserve and pass on to those who come after us. We will be further and further along in becoming technologically enhanced human beings, if not Techno sapiens, so that by then how we view human spirituality, if we do so at all consistent with how we have understood it historically, could very well be of a completely different order. Spiritual qualities such as our compassion, empathy, introspective processing, our relational intelligence and people skills could evolve their way out of who we are becoming as enhanced humans, unless we take great care *in this moment* to hold on to and to foster these precious and fragile gifts. In so doing, we may very well be preserving our unique capacity for a fully embodied experience of divine presence, a direct and contemplative pre-apprehension of God if we put in Rahner's language, before it is mediated and increasingly determined for us by machine intelligence.

It is precisely at this pivotal moment in human history that we find ourselves doing the work of pastoral and spiritual care and therapeutic practice, in a world of dramatic and unrelenting change. Our capacity to effectively care for congregants and clients trying to navigate a world that we all have not yet learned to look at will depend more and more on how familiar we are with the present and future digital landscape and what is before us. For example, what will continue to be at stake for all of us is finding an inner sense of peace and balance, as well as holding on to our spiritual life as human beings, even as we become adept with the new and emerging technologies. Perhaps paradoxically, it is almost as if digital natives already know this, intuitively, and are therefore ahead of the curve, for even if they have never known a world without smartphones and the Internet, they more than previous generations are finding time for contemplative-meditational practice. The regular practice of contemplative prayer and/or mindfulness meditation, as we have learned from neuroscientific studies, can help us cultivate an inner sense of calm and peace, even in the midst of the digital torrent, by literally reducing the neural activity in the stress region of the brain. Over time, we build up, so to speak, more "attention muscle" and greater attentional control, which as we have learned is and will be for some time to come fundamental to navigating the digital terrain in as *human* a way as possible. In looking more closely at the scientific literature, as we will do shortly, we find that working memory and the control of attention can indeed be trained, as we have discovered, a matter of extreme importance for pastoral and spiritual care providers working with anxious digital natives and immigrants.

In a digital world, it will come down more and more to preserving our capacity for attentional control, for we will not be able to hold on to our humanity without it. We already have the timeless wisdom and spiritual practices of various religious traditions at our disposal, even if science is just now confirming the benefits of contemplative-meditational practice. The following story from centuries ago illustrates the point:

> One day a man of the people said to Zen Master Ikkyu: "Master, will you please write for me some maxims of the highest wisdom?"
>
> Ikkyu immediately took his brush and wrote the word "Attention."
>
> "Is that all?" asked the man. "Will you add something more?"
>
> Ikkyu then wrote twice running: "Attention. Attention."
>
> "Well," remarked the man rather irritably, "I really don't see much depth or subtlety in what you have just written."
>
> Then Ikkyu wrote the same word three times running: "Attention. Attention. Attention."
>
> Half angered, the man demanded: "What does that word 'Attention' mean anyway?"
>
> And Ikkyu answered gently: "Attention means attention." (In Kapleau, 1989, p. 11)

Paraphrasing Rahner (1971), in the coming days of the digital revolution, the human person will either be a mystic, experiencing God more directly and contemplatively, or he or she will be nothing at all in any traditional religious or spiritual sense. It is certainly possible that in decades to come the spiritual qualities that have made us human for so long will have evolved their way out of who we are fast becoming, technologically enhanced humans if not a completely different species altogether. Or, perhaps we will find a way to preserve the human spiritual life after all, at least in part through a more informed pastoral and spiritual care that focuses on helping congregants and clients develop greater attentional control by way of contemplative-meditational practice, both during and outside of spiritual-care and psychotherapeutic sessions. Time will tell, and it could very well be less time than we think, given the ever-accelerating advance of technology and machine intelligence. In the end, it will be a matter of whether we value the preservation of human spirituality and wisdom, the "examined life" if we put it in Socratic language, or if we would rather let it up to AI to mostly determine for us, which of course it will if we are doing nothing. To passively wait and see how things will ultimately develop in the new digital world, the extent of our merger with machines, before taking any action on our own as well as on behalf of those in our care would be a serious mistake, for by then the opportunity to help guide the evolutionary process toward loving and compassionate ends will have come and gone. If we do not take full advantage of this pivotal moment in the history of our species, if we are not proactive, the capacity for attentional control and in-depth reflection, fundamental to the preservation and development of the human spiritual life, could evolve its way out of us. By then some of us will have determined, again in Socratic terms, that "the unreflected cyber life may not be worth living" (Delio, 2013, p. 174), only to discover that the opportunity to reflect deeply on what we wanted to preserve about our fundamental humanity will have slipped away.

THE FINDINGS OF CONTEMPLATIVE NEUROSCIENCE

In an earlier publication (Bingaman, 2014), I argued for a paradigm shift in Christian faith communities, whereby we begin elevating contemplative spiritual practice to "a level of comparable importance with religious belief and doctrine" (p. 1). It is certainly ironic that the argument even needs to be made in the first place, given the rich tradition of contemplative wisdom and practice in the history of the church. And yet, so often in recent years contemplative spiritual practice has been relegated to the periphery, at least in the context of *Western* Christianity, as local churches and judicatories go into "survival mode," preoccupied with staying afloat financially, stemming the tide of declining membership, and finding ways to resuscitate and jump-start dying congregations. Nor is it for the most part a central feature of seminary education and preparation for ministry, even with the richness of the historical tradition, as theological schools and ordination committees, aware of the current and challenging social milieu, instead prefer to keep the focus more on developing the seminarian's core religious beliefs, biblical knowledge, theological understanding, and liturgical effectiveness. All important and integral aspects of pastoral ministry, to be sure, and yet this approach to ministerial preparation overlooks the very heart of Christian spirituality, namely cultivating a contemplative spiritual *practice*. "I am not suggesting," writes Ilia Delio (2008), "that we eliminate academic theology, for it serves a vital apologetic function through critique and rigorous questioning; however, I am suggesting that it be complemented by contemplative theology and a development of inwardness" (p. 151). This resonates with my own view, although I would want to take contemplative theology and the development of inwardness a step further, beyond "complementing" academic theology to a more elevated level of *comparable importance*. Too often "contemporary theology has given insufficient attention to many key elements of human life, such as contemplation, silence, and the well-being of the body; yet, these are essential to a renewed cosmic Christology in the third millennium" (Delio, 2008, p. 151). If we put it more in the language of this particular study, we could say that the development of contemplation, silence, and inwardness is essential to a renewed "mystical" faith in the digital world. "We need," adds Delio

(2008), "a return to prayer, solitude, contemplation, and scripture as the source of the spiritual life, and spirituality as the source of theology," for this more than anything offers "a penetrating insight into God as creator, as the God of hope and promise, and the future into which we are moving" (p. 151).

In elevating contemplative practice to a level of comparable importance with religious belief and theological teaching, we are simply being more mindful of the historical richness and fullness of the Christian faith tradition. We are also increasingly aware of the growing body of contemporary neuro-scientific research, which is revealing the psychophysiological benefits of regular contemplative prayer and meditation, above and beyond a penetrating insight into the God of the future. In a rapidly changing digital world, con-templative-meditational practice can no longer be considered optional for pastoral and spiritual practitioners and those in our care, for it is a proven means of finding inner balance and peace and fostering attentional control. It may of course take some getting used to at first, may initially seem counter-intuitive to much of our theological education and training in the context of Western Christianity, which tends to focus more on academic than on any contemplative theology. As I have pointed out before (Bingaman, 2014), in *The Power of Neuroplasticity for Pastoral and Spiritual Care*:

> [Contemplative spirituality] has often been considered the primary domain of the Desert Fathers and Mothers, the Christian mystics, and those engaged in monastic life and religious orders. By contrast, the average Christian congre-gant worshiping in the pews is encouraged to reflect on the essential tenets of the Christian faith, to recite the creeds, and to engage in the collective liturgi-cal rituals of Christian worship often without a similar emphasis on developing a daily spiritual practice. Nor do seminaries, by and large, make contemplative practice a curricular priority for students aspiring to be ministers and pastoral care providers, even in an age when stress and anxiety are on the rise. The paradigmatic turn toward an awareness of the reality of neuroplasticity and the practical implications for pastoral and spiritual care will necessitate a reorder-ing of pastoral and clinical priorities, as we begin to recognize that through a daily practice of contemplative prayer and meditation, the average congregant or client can over time rewire the neural pathways of the brain for the better. By learning to calm the fear and stress region of the brain, we are able to experience more tangibly and fully the peace and joy of God's presence. (pp. 3–4)

The argument for elevating contemplative spiritual practice to a level of comparable importance with religious belief and doctrine is now threefold: (1) the spiritual benefits of a regular contemplative-meditational practice, such as a direct and unmediated experience of divine presence; (2) the psychophysiological benefits, including a reduction of activity in the stress region of the brain; and (3) an enhanced capacity for attentional control and sustained concentration, of particular relevance for human life in a digital world. Andrew Newberg (2009), in studying the longitudinal effects of contemplative prayer, has found that a regular spiritual practice over time can make profound and lasting changes in our consciousness and in our perceptions of the world, by strengthening neural circuitry associated with memory, cognition, and attentiveness (p. 190). His initial research simultaneously focusing on a group of Franciscan nuns practicing the Christian Centering Prayer and a group of Buddhist monks practicing breathing meditation revealed that "activities involving meditation and intensive prayer permanently strengthen neural functioning in specific parts of the brain that are involved with lowering anxiety and depression, enhancing social awareness and empathy, and improving cognitive and intellectual functioning" (Newberg and Waldman, 2009, p. 149). Indeed, a practical way to increase our attentiveness, social awareness, and empathy, supported by research, could not come at a better time, given what is presently at stake for humanity. Newberg (2009) has this to say about his findings:

> This was the first brain-scan study of Christian contemplative practitioners, and we discovered that the neurological changes were significant and very different from how the brain normally functions. Even more surprising, the neurological changes were nearly the same as those we recorded from a group of Buddhist practitioners, who obviously nurtured very different beliefs. This evidence confirmed our hypothesis that the benefits gleaned from prayer and meditation may have less to do with a specific theology than with the ritual techniques of breathing, staying relaxed, and focusing one's attention upon a concept that evokes comfort, compassion, or a spiritual sense of peace. Of course, the more you believe in what you are meditating or praying about, the stronger the response will be. (p. 48)

Newberg is referring to the *physiological* benefits of prayer and meditation, when he says that in all likelihood they may have more to do with certain ritual techniques and practices, with *how* we pray and meditate. This is not to imply that what we believe, religiously and theologically, is unimportant, for if we are praying or meditating about a deeply-held belief, as Newberg indicates the neuroimaging response and activity is more robust. As a medical researcher, he is mindful of the methodological scope of his neuroscientific investigation, and therefore with a focus more on what improves human physiology will yield to pastoral and spiritual practitioners when it comes to determining the most tangible *spiritual* benefits. Notwithstanding the methodological boundaries, and they are important, I would argue that there is a cross-disciplinary synergy between contemplative neuroscience and what Delio (2008) has referred to as contemplative religion or theology. What is fundamental to both, contemplative neuroscience and theology, is that certain forms of prayer, specifically contemplative in nature, ultimately yield physiological *and* spiritual benefits vital for a digital age. Physiologically, writes Newberg (2009), "contemplative practices strengthen a specific neurological circuit that generates peacefulness, social awareness, and compassion for others" (p. 7). Similarly, the very same contemplative practices strengthen a specific "spiritual circuit" that is grounded in a direct experience of divine presence, which enhances what are the most fundamental and, in a digital world, fragile qualities of human existence: an inner sense of peace and well-being, social and relational intelligence, and, as Carrie Doehring (2015) has said, "the embodied experience of compassion" (p. xvi).

What is important to remember is that for all the spiritual and psycho-physiological benefits, contemplative spiritual practice goes very much against the biochemistry of the brain, against certain deeply ingrained neural predispositions. Put more simply, we are *not* hardwired for contemplative spirituality, no matter how good it is for us and how necessary it is fast becoming for holding on to our humanity in a digital world. After all, the human brain, yours and mine, comes with a built-in negativity bias, as I have discussed previously (Bingaman, 2014), and as a result is predisposed more toward anxious awareness than inner peace and calm, more toward attentional breadth than attentional control. In a sense, what we are doing in the context of regular contemplative-meditational practice is using the mind to re-wire the brain, to literally "re-sculpt" the neural pathways of our own brain. For Harari (2017), "this is all the fault of evolution: For countless generations our biochemical system adapted to increasing our chances of survival and reproduction, not our happiness" (p. 37). The same goes for attentional control and an inner sense of peace; these have also taken a backseat in the course of human evolution, reflecting a brain more hyper-focused on our survival than anything else. What are we to do, then, about this evolutionary hand that we have been dealt, which continues to predispose us toward survival at all costs, even if survival in the present digital age could mean, neurologically, having to let go of fundamental aspects of our humanity? There is only one thing that we can do: in a word, *manipulate* our own brain and biochemistry, while we still have a window of time and opportunity. Otherwise, before we know it, machine intelligence will be doing most of the manipulation for us, significantly more than it is doing already. As far as neuroscience is concerned, this is fundamentally what we are doing by way of contemplative spiritual practice, manipulating our own biochemistry and brain for the better, as we intentionally cultivate an inner sense of peace, contentment, and even happiness. From a physiological standpoint, it is clear that "the only way to ensure lasting contentment is by rigging this system" (Harari, 2017, p. 39).

The possibility of "rigging" the neurological system, through the regular practice of contemplative prayer and meditation, is also supported by other research, such as the work of Sara Lazar at Massachusetts General Hospital and Harvard Medical School. Lazar (2013a) has found through extensive brain-scan research that a regular contemplative-meditational practice will over time literally alter not only the functioning but also the structure of a meditator's brain. Her analyses of meditators have revealed, for example, "more gray matter in part of the prefrontal cortex, which is involved in working memory and selective attention" (p. 84). Gray matter consists of neuron cell bodies associated with information processing, "the parts of the brain where neurons talk to each other and where 'thinking' and neural activity actually happen" (Lazar, 2013a, p. 83). It should be noted that within the brain the prefrontal cortex is central to executive functioning and higher-order thinking. If we apply the findings to our own study, to how we plan on navigating the present and future digital terrain in a way that preserves our humanity, it is not too difficult to see that contemplative prayer and meditation offers a useful starting point for enhancing attentional stability. More specifically, Lazar (2013a) has found that contemplative practitioners "are better able to navigate and cope with difficult situations or emotions, and that they have increased empathy and compassion, as well as improved memory and ability to pay attention" (p. 80). She notes that other scientific researchers have been busy putting her claims to the test, so that "good scientific evidence now exists to support some of them, particularly for attention and compassion" (p. 80). For example, Richard Davidson (2012), following extensive research on the impact of compassion meditation on the brain, has discovered a noticeable reduction in neural activity associated with fear, with people who practice this form of meditation regularly developing "a strong disposition to alleviate suffering and to wish others to be happy" (p. 223).

The findings cannot come a minute too soon in a world of social media that favors, as Bermúdez (2017) has said, "spouts" of impulse and aggression over sustained and compassionate reflection. Nor can they come soon enough for pastoral and spiritual practitioners, looking for evidence-based therapeutic methods to help congregants and clients cultivate a sense of inner peace and balance as well as compassionate awareness, grounded in attentional stability. It will require us to elevate contemplative spiritual practice to a level of much greater importance, which reflects a clear understanding of the neuroscientific research and what is ultimately at stake for the religious believer and all human beings in a digital world. It also reflects a clear grasp of contemporary spirituality, with more and more people, digital natives in particular, preferring to be a "mystic" or nothing at all, having a direct and immediate experience of divine presence that is not always mediated by extensive theological and doctrinal rationale. For pastoral and spiritual care to be effective in a digital age, it will need to be less dualistic, less about keeping science separate from religious belief than about, as Ian Barbour (1997) has argued, extending the boundaries of acceptable science and religion to the possibility of new paradigms that are more inclusive. In our work with clients and congregants, we will need to help them strengthen *spiritual* circuitry that is grounded in a more direct experience of God, even as we help them to strengthen *neural* circuitry supporting attentional stability and compassionate awareness. In terms of the latter, working to strengthen specific neural circuitry and even re-sculpt the neural pathways of the brain, we are helping to facilitate the process of neuroplasticity, which for Lazar (2013) "is at the heart of the therapeutic process as well as the learning process" (p. 81). The discovery of neuroplasticity, that the brain is built for change across the entire lifespan, has led Mario Beauregard (2012) to argue for making it a central focus of the therapeutic process. He writes in *Brain Wars*:

> Research has shown that we can intentionally train our minds, through meditative practices, to bolster the activity of regions and circuits of our brains involved not only in attention and concentration, but in empathy, compassion, and emotional well-being. Such mental exercises can even modify the physical structure of the brain. Changes in thoughts, beliefs, and emotions, made in the context of psychotherapy, also have the power to transform the brain, as shown by neuroimaging studies. Additionally, there is now some evidence that mental training can slow down the cognitive decline and reduction in gray matter volume typically seen in normal aging. (pp. 87–88)

CONTEMPLATIVE PASTORAL AND SPIRITUAL CARE

In elevating contemplative spiritual practice to a level of greater importance, it is necessary for pastoral and spiritual practitioners to understand that this will be a paradigm shift in both theory *and* practice. It is not, in other words, only a matter for our theological reflection, as if revising our theological framework is an end in itself. Rather, the contextual pastoral and practical theology we develop for a digital age is ultimately a means to the greater end of directly informing our pastoral and clinical practice, specifically *how* we intend to work with and care for both digital natives and immigrants. It is becoming more apparent that for pastoral and spiritual care to be effective in a digital age, it will need to take very seriously the momentous turn in religious and spiritual orientation toward a more "mystical" and experiential spirituality. Moreover, it will need to grasp the urgency of this pivotal and unprecedented moment in our history, when there is still a window of time and opportunity to preserve the unique aspects of our humanity, before we witness a more complete merger of humans and machines. As we have discussed, this presupposes that we are working to strengthen the neural circuitry associated with attentional control and sustained concentration, our own circuitry as well as that of our clients and congregants. For those who have not practiced contemplative prayer and meditation before, it will more than likely not come naturally at first, for the human brain at the present moment is adapted more toward attentional breadth than to attentional depth and single-pointed concentration. It would be a good idea, then, to help those in our care get started by actually doing contemplative spiritual practices in the context of, for example, the therapy or pastoral-care session, a weekly meditation group, a support group, and so forth before and even after they begin doing them at home. Recall that we are, so to speak, attempting to rig the neurological system, our own brain in fact, and it will take some time for it to rewire accordingly.

In this digital age of immediacy, it will be challenging for more than a few of us to "downshift" neurologically, given our genetic predisposition toward attentional breadth combined with the accelerating pace of digital life. Some in our care, some of us may feel discouraged when it does not happen overnight, when it seems that contemplative-meditational practice requires more time and patience than we can give, particularly when there is so much else we need to be doing. Lizabeth Roemer and Susan Orsillo (2009) want to help us "normalize" this initial feeling, when they write: "If it were easy . . . we would all do it naturally, and clearly we do not" (p. 134). Thus, practitioners do well to empathize with any resistance early on, letting clients and congregants know it is best to "think small," at least in the beginning. Roemer and Orsillo (2009), writing in *Mindfulness- and Acceptance-Based Behavioral Therapies in Practice*, offer a case vignette to illustrate that "while validating doubts clients may have about the potential usefulness of this practice, therapists can ask them to commit to trying some of the prescribed exercises and watching to see whether or not they seem beneficial:"

Client: I just couldn't set aside any time for the practice this week. I have too much else going on.

Therapist: I know how challenging it can be to find extra time. Can you give me an example of a particular day and what happened when you tried to practice [the meditation]?

Client: I thought I would wake up in the morning and do the breathing for a few minutes. . . . But then I started thinking about everything I had to do that day, and I just didn't see how sitting and doing nothing would help at all.

Therapist: So, part of what happened is that it didn't feel like practicing would be useful for you, given everything you have going on. Is that right?

Client: Yeah, I guess so. I mean I understand what you said about how doing this would help me to see my emotions differently, but when I have so many things on my plate, I just don't feel like I can indulge myself in this kind of thing. People are counting on me to do things for them.

Therapist: I really understand that reaction. . . . It's so incredibly hard to feel like sitting and not doing anything will do anything other than give us less time to do all the things we need to. And it can feel selfish. Yet in my experience, when I force myself to take a little time and do these kinds of [meditational] exercises, I actually find that I am able to do the other things I need to do more efficiently and with less distress than if I don't, and I'm able to be with other people and meet their needs better. But it's really hard to trust that, particularly at the beginning. So, in a way, I'm asking you if you can take a leap of faith and just do these practices, even if they feel like a waste of time, for a couple of weeks. . . . What about trying to practice for only five minutes a day this coming week?

Client: Really? Is that enough time?

Therapist: The main thing is to start to develop this new habit. And it's a hard habit to develop. It's much better to practice for five minutes regularly than to set your goals so high that you don't do it at all.

Client: I can definitely do five minutes.

Therapist: OK, remember you're still probably going to feel it's a waste of time. And you might still feel that after you practice. It might be boring or anxiety-provoking, or you might feel bad at it and think, "Why did she tell me to do this?" Do you think you can stick with it even if all of those things happen?

Client: Yeah, I can do anything for five minutes (pp. 134–135).

In terms of *what* specific contemplative-meditational practices to introduce to those in our care, this will depend somewhat on the faith tradition of the particular client or congregant. Recall that in the context of Newberg's study, the Franciscan nuns were practicing the *Christian* Centering Prayer, whereas the Buddhist monks were practicing something more in keeping with their religious or spiritual orientation, namely breathing meditation. As far as the brain is concerned, the contemplative practices coming from very different spiritual traditions strengthen the same neural circuitry, although as Newberg pointed out the circuitry will be strengthened all the more if we actually *believe* in what we are praying or meditating about. That said, there are also meditational practices that work across many if not all faith traditions, and even with those who eschew any organized religious framework, the growing percentage of digital natives who would rather self-identify as "spiritual but not religious" (SBNR). Indeed, some of these practices have the potential of helping us hold on to our humanity in a digital age, or more specifically hold on to certain precious and increasingly fragile qualities that make us human, such as our compassion and empathy and good-humored decency. As we noted, a growing body of research on the impact of compassion meditation on the brain is revealing that people who practice this form of meditation develop a *strong* disposition to reduce suffering and to wish that others be happy, including those that we like and get along with *and* those that we do not. Moreover, we are also learning from the research that the regular practice of compassion meditation reduces attentional distraction or what is referred to as "mind wandering." For example, an important study conducted several years ago at Stanford University's Center for Compassion and Altruism Research and Education (CCARE) provided strong support that "compassion training can reduce mind wandering and elicit caring behaviors for oneself and others" (Jazaieri *et al.*, 2016). Compassion meditation is therefore distinct from other contemplative-meditational practices, in that it "involves the recognition of, and wish to relieve, suffering in others and oneself," with "the focus of one's attention on a particular person, object, or situation" (Parker, 2015). In another study, at the Center for Healthy Minds at the University of Wisconsin-Madison, researchers found that even after two weeks, individuals who participated in compassion-meditation training were "more altruistic toward a victim after witnessing an unfair social inter-action" (Weng *et al.*, 2013). Out of the research conducted, Helen Weng and her team have developed a "Compassion Meditation Script," a practical tool that can be used in our work with congregants and clients, helping them to develop simultaneously attentional control *and* compassionate awareness. Below is an abridged version of the meditation:

Compassion for a loved one:

After settling into a comfortable and relaxed position, picture someone who is close to you, someone that you feel a great amount of love towards. Now think of a time when this person was suffering. Maybe they experienced an illness, an injury, or a difficult time in a relationship. Notice how you feel when you think of his or her suffering. How does your heart feel? Do you feel warmth, openness and tenderness? Are there other sensations, perhaps an aching sensation? Recite silently to him or her: "May you be free from this suffering, May you have joy and happiness."

Compassion for self:

Contemplate a time when you have suffered yourself. Perhaps you experienced a conflict with someone you care about, or did not succeed in something you wanted, or were physically ill. Notice how you feel when you think of your suffering. How does your heart feel? Do you continue to feel warmth, openness and tenderness? Are there other sensations, perhaps an aching sensation? Just as we wish for our loved one's suffering to end, we wish that our own suffering would end. Silently recite to yourself: "May I be free from this suffering, May I have joy and happiness."

Compassion for a neutral person:

Now visualize someone you neither like nor dislike, but someone you may see in your everyday life, such as a classmate you are not familiar with, a bus driver, or a stranger you pass on the street. Although you are not familiar with this person, think of how this person may suffer in his or her own life. This person may also have conflicts with loved ones, or struggled with an addiction, or may have suffered illness. Imagine a situation in which this person may have suffered.

Notice your heart center . . . does it feel different? Do you feel more warmth, openness and tenderness? Are there other sensations, perhaps an aching sensation? How does your heart feel different from when you were envisioning your own or a loved one's suffering? See if it can be as strong as the wish for your own or a loved one's suffering to be relieved. Silently recite to him or her: "May you be free from this suffering, May you have joy and happiness."

Compassion for an enemy:

Now visualize someone you have difficulty with in your life. This may be a parent you disagree with, an ex-girlfriend or boyfriend, a roommate you had an argument with, or a coworker you do not get along with. Although you may have negative feelings towards this person, think of how this person has suffered in his or her own life. This person has also had conflicts with loved ones, or has dealt with failures, or may have suffered illness. Think of a situation in which this person may have suffered.

Notice your heart center . . . does it feel different? Do you feel more warmth, openness and tenderness? Are there other sensations, perhaps an aching sensation? How does your heart feel different from when you were envisioning your own or a loved one's suffering? See if it can be as strong as the wish for your own or a loved one's suffering to be relieved. Silently recite to him or her:

"May you be free from this suffering, May you have joy and happiness."

Compassion for all beings:

Now end with a wish for all other beings' suffering to be relieved. Just as we wish to have peace, happiness, and to be free from suffering, so do all beings. Bask in the joy of this open-hearted wish to ease the suffering of all people and how this attempt brings joy, happiness, and compassion in your heart at this very moment. (Weng *et al.*, 2013)

In the context of Christian faith communities, pastoral and spiritual care providers will perhaps want to consider first and foremost the modern Centering Prayer method put forward by Fr. Thomas Keating (2006), which the Franciscan nuns were practicing in Newberg's (2009) study. It can be practiced for five minutes a day, or for ten minutes or twenty minutes or longer, depending on the particular client or congregant. It is not at all complicated, but rather in a way profound in its simplicity, even if at first the "centering" of our attention can feel a bit unnatural and counterintuitive. We are, once again, attempting to rig the neurological system, to rewire a brain that has steadily adapted to the bombardment of digital data and information. Pastoral and spiritual practitioners will therefore have to "normalize" any initial hesitation or even resistance to contemplative spiritual practice from clients and congregants, in a manner that is consistent with the therapeutic intervention in the case vignette. In terms of practicing the Centering Prayer in a digital culture, we must keep in mind that at least initially, as Cynthia Bourgeault (2016) has said, "it is not hard to do, but it is hard—at first—to value" (p. 13). She notes that "the method of Centering Prayer consists in learning to withdraw attention from our thoughts—those incessant creations of our busy minds—in order to rest in a gentle, open attentiveness to divine reality itself" (p. 13). In all likelihood it will not feel natural or "normal," not at first, for what is valued more in a digital world is perpetual focus on external stimuli, for fear of missing out (FOMO) on some bit of ephemeral information. If we put this in the "mystical" language of Rahner (1971), the contemplative practice of Centering Prayer, above and beyond helping us cultivate attentional control of our busy minds, offers us the possibility of resting in an open attentiveness to and pre-apprehension of divine presence and infinite being. Centering Prayer, then, takes us beyond "the 'standard model' of meditation," ultimately beyond strengthening the powers of selective attention by way of the breath or a sacred word or mantra toward, as Bourgeault (2016) puts it so well, "the release of attention or perhaps, more accurately, its reconfiguration" (p. 2).

The Centering Prayer method, which offers the potential for stabilizing and reconfiguring attention, is rather easy to remember even if the actual practice of it, *doing* Centering Prayer, is more challenging at least in the beginning. Briefly summarizing and paraphrasing the method of Keating (2006), we begin by choosing a sacred word or mantra that has deep resonance and meaning, which symbolizes our openness to divine presence; sitting comfortably, we let the word or mantra come to mind, even in rhythmic measure to the breath; and when distracting thoughts intrude, the incessant creations of our busy minds, we simply return ever so gently and as often as needed to our attentional "anchor," the sacred word or mantra (p. 122). From the perspective of neuroscience, returning "ever so gently" or *non-judgmentally* to the attentional anchor, whether it be the sacred word or the breath, is pivotal to developing attentional control and sustained concentration. As intrusive thoughts and feelings and memories come to mind, during our spiritual practice, we learn to observe their coming and going "as just the exudations of [our] brain's synapses and action potentials" (Davidson, 2012, p. 201). We do not, in other words, judge how well we are keeping our focus, or how poorly for that matter, in this case with the practice of Centering Prayer. Newberg (2009) is clear that "the worst thing you can do in meditation is to critically judge your performance . . . self-criticism stimulates the amygdala, which releases myriad stress-provoking neurochemicals and hormones" (p. 195). Put more spiritually, in returning ever so gently and non-judgmentally to the sacred word or mantra, as intrusive and unwanted thoughts arise, we are creating the space where we can rest in an open attentiveness to divine mystery and reality. To help facilitate this resting in a gentle and open attentiveness to God's loving presence, by way of Centering Prayer, Keating (2006) offers us the following reflective meditation:

We begin our prayer by disposing our body. Let it be relaxed and calm, but inwardly alert.

The root of prayer is interior silence. We may think of prayer as thoughts or feelings expressed in words. But this is only one expression. Deep prayer is the laying aside of thoughts. It is the opening of mind and heart, body and feelings—our whole being—to God, the Ultimate Mystery, beyond words, thoughts, and emotions. We do not resist them or suppress them. We accept them as they are and go beyond them, not by effort, but by letting them all go by. We open our awareness to the Ultimate Mystery whom we know by faith is within us, closer than breathing, closer than thinking, closer than choosing—closer than consciousness itself. The Ultimate Mystery is the ground in which our being is rooted, the Source from whom our life emerges at every moment.

We are totally present now with the whole of our being, in complete openness, in deep prayer. The past and future—time itself—are forgotten. We are here in the presence of the Ultimate Mystery. Like the air we breathe, this divine presence is all around us and within us, distinct from us, but never separate from us. We may sense this Presence drawing us from within, as if touching our spirit and embracing it, or carrying us beyond ourselves into pure awareness.

We surrender to the attraction of interior silence, tranquility, and peace. We do not try to feel anything, reflect about anything. Without effort, without trying, we sink into this Presence, letting everything else go. Let love alone speak: the simple desire to be one with the Presence, to forget self, and to rest in the Ultimate Mystery.

This Presence is immense, yet so humble; awe-inspiring, yet so gentle; limitless, yet so intimate, tender and personal. I know that I am known. Everything in my life is transparent in this Presence. It knows everything about me—all my weaknesses, brokenness, sinfulness—and still loves me infinitely. This Presence is healing, strengthening, refreshing—just by its Presence. It is nonjudgmental, self-giving, seeking no reward, boundless in compassion. It is like coming home to a place I should never have left, to an awareness that was somehow always there, but which I did not recognize. I cannot force this awareness, or bring it about. A door opens within me, but from the other side. I seem to have tasted before the mysterious sweetness of this enveloping, permeating Presence. It is both emptiness and fullness at once.

We wait patiently; in silence, openness, and quiet attentiveness; motionless within and without. We surrender to the attraction to be still, to be loved, just to *be*. (pp. 129–130)

Chapter Six

A Mindfulness-Informed Framework and Approach

In the final chapter I want to develop a therapeutic framework for situating the work of pastoral and spiritual care, as well as clinical practice, in a digital age. We have established that with the accelerated advance of digital technologies and artificial intelligence, it will be a challenge to maintain the human capacity for attentional stability and sustained concentration. In fact, it already *is* a challenge, as the digital culture continues to intensify with increasing speed and power. Nor is there any going back to a simpler pre-digital way of living, for even as I am writing this, the "train" of digital progress is fast leaving the station. And, as Harari (2017) has suggested, it could very well be the last train to leave the "station" we have called Homo sapiens, before we make the transition to Techno sapiens. Even now we are becoming a biological-technological hybridity, metaphoric cyborgs if we put it in the language of Ilia Delio (2008). And, as we continue to traverse the coming decades of the twenty-first century, we will likely witness a more complete human-machine merger. We have before us a window of time and opportunity to preserve what has made and still continues to make us uniquely human, such as our consciousness-based introspective processing, our compassion and empathy, our relational intelligence and "people skills," all of which hinges on our ability to preserve and maintain something even more fundamental, namely the capacity for attentional stability. But, given the accelerated advance of the digital culture, the window of opportunity will not remain open indefinitely, and could begin closing faster than we think. In the realm of pastoral and spiritual care, we can help to guide the process forward toward more compassionate and loving ends, by making attentional control more of a central focus in our work with clients and congregants. This assumes the elevation of contemplative-meditational practice to a place of greater importance, for as we are learning from contemplative neuroscience it is spiritual *practice* more than anything that has the potential to keep the human brain focused in the midst of the digital tsunami. The neuroscientific findings have even prompted the emergence of recent therapies that are intent on making the development of attentional control central to the therapeutic process. These so-called "third-wave" cognitive therapies, mindfulness-based approaches in particular, will serve as an important reference point and framework for situating the work of pastoral and spiritual care in a digital age.

THE DOING AND BEING MODES OF MIND

There are several mindfulness-based therapies that intentionally make meditational practice a core feature of the therapeutic work, both within and outside of counseling sessions. For example, Dialectical Behavior Therapy (DBT), originally developed to treat borderline personality disorder, uses mindfulness meditation to help clients learn to better regulate their emotional distress. Another approach is Acceptance and Commitment Therapy (ACT), which through various mindfulness practices, including meditation, similarly helps a client to tolerate or *accept* the moment-to-moment fluctuation of moods, thoughts, and emotions, even if she does not always *like* what she is experiencing. Acceptance, as we have discussed, is not synonymous with "liking;" rather, the client learns over time that she does not have to immediately react to this thought or that feeling, that she does not necessarily have to *do* anything about it other than *be* mindfully aware of what she is experiencing in the present moment. The distinction between doing and being, or more precisely the doing and being modes of mind, is what distinguishes another third-wave cognitive approach: Mindfulness-Based Cognitive Therapy (MBCT). Building on the Mindfulness-Based Stress Reduction (MBSR) model, which was designed to help people, more specifically hospital patients cope with the stress and anxiety stemming from chronic pain and illness, MBCT was originally put forward to treat the relapse and recurrence of depression. It is well known that with depression, there can often be considerable "doing" in the form of rumination, as we try to "think" our way out of feeling unhappy and paradoxically keep ourselves "locked into the state of mind from which we are doing our best to escape" (Segal *et al.*, 2013, p. 66). In the context of MBCT, clients learn to develop attentional stability by way of mindfulness meditation, so that they can begin observing, nonjudgmentally, their own ruminative thinking. Over time and through *regular* contemplative-meditational practice, both during *and* outside of therapy sessions, clients learn to "step out of the 'automatic pilot' state of mind in order to nip in the bud the escalation of self-sustaining patterns of depressive thought" (Segal *et al.*, 2013, pp. 50–51). As we learned earlier, this uses much of the client's capacity for attentional processing, so that little remains for anxious and depressive rumination. The MBCT approach is therefore

> Directly concerned with teaching people to decenter from their thoughts and emotions without avoiding, denying, or suppressing them. It teaches close observation of these phenomena and thus discourages experiential avoidance. It also teaches nonjudgmental acceptance and non-reactivity to these phenomena. (Coffman *et al.*, 2006, p. 34)

Sometimes there is an assumption that the therapeutic technique of "decentering" from thoughts and feelings encourages clients to detach from their experience, creating as it were an emotional if not disembodied disconnect. The assumption is unfortunate and stands in need of immediate reassessment. Decentering, analogously known as "reperceiving," helps clients intentionally focus their attention on present-moment experience, by developing so to speak an "observing self" that is metacognitively aware of the "experiencing self" in any given moment. Detachment or disconnect is in sharp contrast with the actual experience of decentering or reperceiving, which whether applied in the therapy session and/or in everyday life has the potential to engender "a deep knowing and intimacy with whatever arises moment by moment" (Shapiro & Carlson, 2017, p. 104). Moreover, it offers the client a needed "sacred pause" from life on auto-pilot, from the accelerated "doing mode" that is fast becoming our normal baseline in a digital world. Decentering, then, does not translate as disconnection or dissociation from one's embodied experience, but instead "simply allows one to deeply experience each event of the mind and body without identifying with or clinging to it" (Shapiro & Carlson, 2017, p. 104). We do not, in other words, have to *do* anything with a thought or feeling that comes to mind, other than to be mindfully aware that it has now entered our awareness.

For mindfulness-based cognitive therapies, this represents something of a departure from the more familiar cognitive-behavioral therapy (CBT), which does encourage clients to *do* something about their thoughts and feelings, particularly those that are anxious and depressive, to engage the irrational thoughts in what is known as "cognitive disputation." If, for example, a client tends to cognitively fuse with her anxious thoughts about being a good mother, prompting a chain reaction of catastrophizing when remembering all the times that she has failed her children, the CBT practitioner will encourage the anxious mother to directly challenge and dispute her own irrational thinking. In contrast, the MBCT practitioner would not encourage the mother to *do* anything, other than to be deeply aware and mindful of what she is experiencing in the present moment, and more compassionate with herself. This represents an intentional therapeutic shift away from *doing* toward *being*, as "doing" in the form of cognitively disputing with ourselves will likely fire up the stress region of the brain, triggering the release of stress-provoking neurochemicals. Put another way, *doing* in the form of cognitive disputation could be counterproductive if we are not careful, when viewed from the standpoint of neuroscience, a finding that clearly guides the practice of mindfulness-based therapies. Thus, in the context of MBCT, "no attempt is made to evaluate the rationality of observed thoughts or to dispute or change their content" (the CBT approach), for the mindful approach to thoughts and feelings simply encourages a direct observation and "acceptance" of what *is* in the present moment, which "slows reactivity to mood, increasing time and ability to choose new responses" (Coffman *et al.*, 2006, p. 35). Clients begin to change the way they *relate* to their internal experience, learning how to simply let it be, letting passing thoughts and feelings come and go without having to do anything.

How does the mindful approach to therapy, and by extension the mindful approach to pastoral and spiritual care, apply to the present discussion of human life in a rapidly changing digital world, driven by the accelerated advance of digital technologies, social media, and artificial intelligence? In the Western world, it is well known that historically far more emphasis and value have been given to doing than being, starting long before there was the slightest hint of a computer age. Notwithstanding the rich contemplative tradition of the Christian faith, which would encourage the regular practice of learning to simply *be* grounded and centered in the presence of God, the church in the West has often supported and even privileged the work ethic of *doing*, the hallmark of Western capitalism. Christian believers have value to the extent that they *do*, to the extent they are productive and not idle. Even Scripture seems to support the "work ethic" of doing, at least a *very* loose and we might add inaccurate translation of the sacred text: "Idle hands are the devil's workshop" (Proverbs 16:27). After centuries of elevating *doing* in society, the church, the educational system, it is safe to assume that it is firmly woven into the fabric of Western culture, not to mention into the hardwiring of the Western individual.

Not that doing is necessarily a bad thing; a certain amount of productivity and creativity is obviously fundamental to human evolution and the flourishing of human culture. The problem is when the doing goes to our head, in the form of excessive mental chatter, problem-solving, and simply needing perpetual mental stimulation, the latter most certainly heightened by our living on the "screen." Thus, while the cognitive skills of doing and producing and problem-solving are highly valued in our culture, "the doing mode of mind," as Rebecca Crane (2017) has rightly observed, "can tip from being a functional, adaptive orientation (i.e., one that helps us skillfully navigate through the logistics, problems, and challenges of our lives), into a driven-doing mode" (p. 22). Mindfulness-based therapies focus on helping clients "step out" of and decenter from the mental turbulence and fatigue associated with doing mode, to learn to experience a very different mode in the form of being, even if only for a brief moment initially. Over time and with regular meditational practice, it is possible to find a more optimal balance between doing and being, even in a digital world. Crane (2017) adds that "given that the majority of people (particularly in Western cultures) are trained to operate predominately in doing mode, and that the problematic patterns of mind, which are the target of MBCT, arise and proliferate within doing mode, the overriding emphasis in [MBCT] is to facilitate participants in experiencing being mode" (p. 26).

We have noted that the human brain is an extraordinary adaptation and anticipation machine, capable of habituating to any environment it encounters, which is something of a double-edged sword. On the one hand, it supports our efforts to navigate the terrain before us in every time and place, and is therefore singularly focused on our immediate and future survival as individuals and as a species. On the other hand, this can only mean that it is far less invested in the being mode of mind, and in keeping us centered in the present moment of experience by way of attentional depth and concentration. From a neurological standpoint, experiencing the being mode of mind, either as practitioners or as clients and congregants, goes against the grain, for we as human beings are clearly hardwired for *doing*, just as we are neurologically hardwired for anxious awareness. The human brain, in other words, yours and mine, is focused first and foremost on motivating us to *do*, in anticipation of what may lie ahead in the future, both short- and long-term. Mindfulness and/or contemplative spiritual practice, then, reflecting the being mode of mind, will not come naturally for the human brain, nor will resting in the gift of the present moment, if we recall Jesus' teaching (Matthew 6:34). While Jesus obviously was not using mindfulness terminology in the Sermon on the Mount, specifically the modes of mind put forward by MBCT, in a way he is similarly encouraging a shift away from ingrained human experience on autopilot, from the busy doing mode of mind that is forever trying to anticipate the future to the being mode of mind that learns through regular spiritual practice to be more grateful for the gift of today.

If the being mode of mind has always gone against the grain, neurologically counter to the hardwiring of the human brain and central nervous system, we can only imagine the extent to which the challenge is now amplified as we continue to make our way in a digital world. Indeed, the brain's orientation to doing and to anticipating the future can only be in a steady if not exponential state of upshift, as we try to navigate uncharted territory and the unprecedented landscape of digital technologies and machine intelligence. To state the obvious, with the continued proliferation of digital data and information, it is impossible to even remotely keep up with it all. As we discussed earlier, by way of Torkel Klingberg's (2009) research, the brain we have today is remarkably similar and almost identical to the "stone-age brain" of thousands of years ago, only now the same brain has to take on, let alone process and make meaning of, the torrent of digital information that comes its way, day after day after day. Not that it keeps us from trying, from living with the illusion that we are sufficiently equipped to deal with life on the screen, that we *can* somehow keep up with the digital flow on all of our electronic devices. But in no time the feeling of missing out, missing something important in the form of social-media updates and messages, alerts from the world of politics and finance and entertainment, the latest pop-up bargains from retail advertisers, and so forth begins to enter and quickly pervade our awareness. The fear of missing out (FOMO) has hijacked our awareness to such an extent that we feel we are not doing enough, that we need to do more and keep up with more and more digital data and information in order to be happy. But this is ultimately an illusion, given the present evolutionary state of the human brain, with studies revealing that this particular form of doing mode in the context of digital culture is making us feel more anxious, depressed, and *unhappy*. Mai-Ly Steers (2014) and her colleagues, for example, writing in the paper, "Seeing everyone's highlight reels: How Facebook usage is linked to depressive symptoms," were able to identify a clear link between high use of social media and mental health risk, particularly for youth and young adults, which at bottom has to do with the frequent if not incessant "social comparisons" that we are making anytime we are on the screen:

> A major contribution of the present research is that it provides evidence that computer-mediated interactions on Facebook may indeed negatively impact users' psychological health. Moreover, these studies found that spending more time on Facebook and/or viewing Facebook more frequently, provides people with the opportunity to spontaneously engage in Facebook social comparisons (of any kind), which in turn, is associated with greater depressive symptoms. This pattern of higher depressive symptoms after engaging in Facebook social comparisons may be especially true for college students since they may still be struggling to establish their identities apart from their families, and consequently, may be more susceptible to peer influences. Thus, the current research holds important implications for general populations and, in particular, college students who are depressed and might also be addicted to Facebook. (p. 728)

The implications are significant for a more focused and contextualized approach to pastoral and spiritual care in a digital age, as well as for mental health care in in general. Helping clients and congregants, helping ourselves to downshift from the busy doing mode of mind on the digital "screen" to a more centered being mode has the potential to expand the window of time and opportunity for us to more intentionally hold on to our humanity, as we give careful attention and in-depth reflection to the human qualities we want to preserve in a cyberworld. But again, this presupposes that we can maintain and perhaps even enhance our capacity for attentional control and sustained concentration, which is and will continue to be fundamental to the preservation of human identity, relationality, and spirituality. If we lose it, the capacity for attentional stability, and there is already some indication that it has started to decline, we will also begin losing the qualities that have made us uniquely human for so long, such as our introspective processing and reflection, our compassionate awareness, and our relational and social intelligence. Building on the therapeutic approach of Mindfulness-Based Cognitive Therapy (MBCT), pastoral and spiritual practitioners can begin to see that "the basic tool to effect this change of mental modes, or shift of mental gears, is the intentional use of attention and awareness in particular ways" (Segal, *et al.*, 2013, p. 74). I would also argue that the change effected, from a driven-doing mode to a more attentive being mode, is not only mental but also fundamentally spiritual too, as we cultivate a more contemplative orientation. Not that we ever get entirely beyond doing mode, given our brain's evolutionary predisposition. Even in the context of our contemplative-meditational practice, we must be careful that our meditation and/or contemplative prayer is more in the form of being than in doing mode, not driven by the "goal" of being a more relaxed and spiritual person. As Zindel Segal and the other founders (2013) of MBCT point out, "it is possible for one to try to meditate with so much focus on being someone who gets into a deeply relaxed state that if anything interrupts it, one feels angry and frustrated" (p. 74).

NOT LOOKING THE OTHER WAY

We are at a crossroads in human history, a pivotal moment when we are about to take an unprecedented evolutionary leap forward into completely uncharted territory, when the historical reference points that have guided human development for millennia increasingly have less relevance for how and where we go from here. And, it is only the beginning, as technology continues to extend its influence and power the world over as the dominant organizing force in the evolutionary process. Sometimes there is the argument that technology, machine intelligence, and smartphones are more the reality of the developed Western world, but not as much of an issue in the less developed nations of the Third World. This is another uninformed assumption that stands in need of immediate reassessment, as I witnessed first-hand in 2018, trekking in remote and isolated areas of northwestern Nepal along the Tibetan border. For example, in the *very* remote and completely off-the-grid Himalayan region of Dolpo, far removed from the rest of the world, West *and* East, I was stunned to see the ubiquity of digital devices in the hands of Dolpo farmers plowing the fields, herders guiding yak caravans, women preparing meals for family and trekking guests at isolated campsites in the middle of nowhere, and children and youth focused on their digital games and social media apps. To repeat, and this is more fact than hyperbole, technology is rapidly extending its influence and power the *world over* as the dominant organizing force in the evolutionary process, and it is only going to get even more powerful and dominant in the coming years. Given the extended reach and power of digital technologies, the moment of time and opportunity is *now* before us and not somewhere off in the future, to take full advantage of preserving the very best qualities of human experience.

Even then, it is not entirely clear the extent to which we will be able to hold on to our humanity, as we continue merging with machine intelligence. It ultimately depends on whether we can and will preserve the capacity for attentional control and mindful awareness, a fact of no small importance for the practice of pastoral and spiritual care. At the moment, we are enamored with our sophisticated digital tools and devices, and will continue to be for the foreseeable future, which tend to reinforce our predisposition for attentional breadth over depth by keeping us focused on the rapid and torrential flow of digital information. And yet, whatever the problematic side of our digital devices, and there is certainly a problematic side that poses an existential risk, they are as David Levy (2016) has observed in his important book, *Mindful Tech*, here to stay because "they are undeniably powerful and useful—and in today's world increasingly necessary" (p. 2). Our digital tools, in other words, like technology in general and machine intelligence in particular, can be an existential risk *and/or* an existential opportunity, depending on how *we* as human beings put them to use. Levy (2016) adds:

> The challenge we now face boils down to this: Our devices have vastly extended our attentional choices, but the human attentional capacity remains unchanged (some would even argue that it has actually shrunk). And so we must figure out how to make wise choices, and to figure out what constitutes a wise choice, so we can use our digital tools to their best advantage, and to ours. . . . We function more effectively and more healthfully online when we are attentive, relaxed, and emotionally balanced. This can also be stated in the negative: We operate less effectively and less healthfully when we are distracted, physically uncomfortable, and emotionally upset. And many of us now are often distracted and stressed out when we are online. (p. 3)

Given our neural predisposition for breadth over depth, amplified exponentially by a frenetic digital culture, becoming more attentive, relaxed, and emotionally and I would add spiritually balanced will not come about through cognitive insight alone nor through any act of human willpower, individual or collective. The human brain and the digital technologies it is increasingly merging with are much too powerful as a combined force, to the extent that it is an illusion to think that we can hold on to our human identity and spirituality by merely willing it. Rather, in a digital world it will take something above and beyond a familiar appeal to the human will, a fact of extreme importance for individuals, human society, and for religious faith communities. What is urgently needed at present are spiritual and therapeutic methods that foster first and foremost attentional control and stability, for if the human attentional capacity continues to "shrink," or even if it remains unchanged for that matter, in a digital world it will *not* be possible to hold on to what we have come to value most about our common humanity. If we take inventory of the great variety of therapeutic frameworks and methods potentially at our disposal, there is none that focuses on the stabilization of attention and concentration quite like mindfulness-based cognitive approaches. For the mindfulness-based clinical practitioner, and by extension the mindfulness-informed pastoral and spiritual practitioner, it is the regular *practice* of contemplative prayer and meditation that enhances our attentional capacity, which a growing body of neuroscientific research would support. There is now ample evidence from neurological research that a regular practice of mindfulness meditation and/or contemplative prayer "improves our ability to pay attention in a concentrated and sustained manner," for it "can help us recover more quickly from distractions" (Morgan *et al.*, 2013, p. 78). To be sure, the distractions, particularly those that are *digital*, are increasing exponentially for the average human individual and will continue to increase with no sign of letting up, pushing our psychological, spiritual, *and* attentional capacities to their limits. Recall the earlier discussion of the "cognitive cost" of even a single digital distraction, a fourfold increase of our precious time needed to complete the task we were focused on originally. And, this is without even trying to count the relational cost for individuals and families and for society as a whole, which we can rightly assume is equally costly if not more.

The term *mindfulness*, defined as "moment-by-moment awareness," can be used by clinical and/or religious and spiritual practitioners to "describe a theoretical *construct* (the idea of mindfulness), *practices* for cultivating mindfulness (such as meditation), or psychological *processes* (mechanisms of action in the mind and brain)" (Germer, 2013, p. 6). Put together, the various descriptions can all contribute to and coalesce more generally into a mindfulness-based framework for pastoral and spiritual care, even as they do with more clinical precision for Mindfulness-Based Cognitive Therapy. In the context of mindfulness-informed pastoral and spiritual care, practitioners can encourage the regular if not daily practice of contemplative prayer with congregants and clients, the Christian Centering Prayer for example, having the knowledge that over time contemplative spirituality can and does have above and beyond the spiritual benefits a profound and beneficial impact on psycho-physiological processes and the neural mechanisms of action and change in the mind and brain. In the context of contemplative-meditational practice, both inside and outside the therapy as well as the pastoral- and spiritual-care session, we learn to use the mind to change the brain, which in turn can help us more effectively regulate the steady rush of digital information. More fundamentally, we learn to focus our attention, and to increase our attentional capacity. Mindfulness practice, in its various shapes and forms, is by nature deeply spiritual and embodied, always focused on what is occurring in the present moment of one's *lived* experience by way of the "sacred pause:"

> Mindfulness must be experienced to be known. People may practice mindfulness with varying degrees of intensity. At one end of a continuum of practice is everyday mindfulness. Even in our often pressured and distracted daily lives, it is possible to have mindful moments. We can momentarily disengage from our activities by taking a long, conscious breath, gathering our attention, and then asking ourselves,
>   "What am I sensing in my body right now?"
>   "What am I feeling?"
>   "What am I thinking?"
>   "What is vivid and alive in my awareness?" (Germer, 2013, p. 8)

It therefore becomes a way of life after a while, extending our contemplative-meditational focus beyond the spiritual practice itself to life in general throughout the day, for example when we feel "stressed out" trying to pay the monthly bills, feeling frustrated and angry when traffic is at a standstill and we are late for an important meeting, when we are hurt by the comments of a friend or loved one, *and* when we feel our attention slipping away as we try to keep up with all the digital alerts, updates, messages, and "breaking news." Contemplative-meditational practice, then, even though it can and often does reduce the level of activity in the stress region of the brain, is not as Jon Kabat-Zinn (2011) has noted merely a relaxation technique or even a "technique" at all, but rather "a way of being and of seeing" that rests on a foundation of deep inquiry into the very nature of self and of life (p. 43). Kabat-Zinn (2011), the founder of Mindfulness-Based Stress Reduction (MBSR), the precursor to Mindfulness-Based Cognitive Therapy (MBCT), recounts from years of applying MBSR in his medical practice that he would often hear patients say to him, "Wait a minute! [Mindfulness meditation] isn't stress reduction; this is my whole life!" (p. 43). Whether in the form of meditation and/or contemplative prayer, mindfulness practice becomes a way of life after a while, creating over time a completely different orientation that reflects more of a *being* than a doing mode, a contemplative mode if we put it more spiritually. And, preparatory to the shift toward being or contemplative mode, it creates "deep psychological changes that promote sustained attention," increasing our awareness of the issues and circumstances that have the potential to "hijack our attention and distract us from the therapeutic endeavor" (Morgan *et al.*, 2013, p. 79).

This is a matter of fundamental importance in a digital world, where the attentional focus of both caregiver and care receiver alike is ever being "hijacked," to one degree or another, by the steady flow of digital distractions. For pastoral and spiritual care that is informed by a mindfulness-based therapeutic framework, there is the potential to help our clients and congregants, not to mention ourselves as practitioners, learn to more intentionally "receive the vicissitudes of life with equanimity and insight" (Morgan *et al.*, 2013, p. 78), in particular the "digital vicissitudes" that come to us perpetually in the form of unrelenting digital stimuli. We develop, as Jaco Hamman (2017) has put it, "technological intelligence," something that we will surely need in this evolutionary transition from Homo to Techno sapiens, which is the art of mindfully discerning "the impact of technology on oneself as well as one's relationships with the self, the O/other, culture, and nature while engaging and being able to evaluate digital and virtual content and objects" (p. 13). There is no going back to a simpler time and place, imagined or even real for that matter, to life completely off the grid from the world of digital technologies, as I witnessed firsthand in one of the most remote places on the planet, the Himalayan region of Dolpo in Nepal. It does not get anymore off the grid than in the Dolpo. The reach of computer technology and machine learning is advancing at a far more accelerated pace than most of us realize, and it will not be slowing down anytime soon. Even if we could slow it down a bit, or even manage to put a stop to the rapid advance of digital technologies, as we have seen this would result in an immediate collapse of the national and global economy. Technology and machine intelligence have become so integral to the evolutionary process, the primary driving force in fact, that we can now say with certainty that as technology goes, so will go global economics. All the more reason, as Jaco Hamman (2017) urges, for us to develop increasing "technological intelligence" in this digital age and world, whatever we may think of and however we may feel about the digitization of human life and culture.

This is a pivotal moment in human history, with a window of time and opportunity to very carefully reflect on how we intend to go about navigating the uncharted landscape before us, even as we work to help guide the evolutionary process toward just and compassionate ends. As we approach an unprecedented "tipping point" that is, so to speak, just up ahead, whether it be the middle or latter part of this century or even into the next century, we are, as the MIT researcher Max Tegmark (2018) has said, "the guardians of the future of life now as we shape the age of AI" (p. 335). But the moment as we have discussed will not last forever, or even all that long given the accelerated advance and reach of machine learning. Before we know it the "window" will have come and gone, so that as Harari (2017) has argued we would do well to better understand what is happening, technologically, and make up our minds about it before it makes up more of our minds for us. We have entered "crunch time," in the words of Nick Bostrom (2016), even if the intelligence explosion is still decades away, so that we cannot sit idly by waiting for the digital age to come and go, to run its course. It may be a very long time before the age of artificial intelligence is come and gone, if ever. Nor can we as pastoral and spiritual practitioners look the other way, because we do not like the turn toward a more digital world and culture, hoping and praying that somehow, someway things will work out for the best, that perhaps God will still intervene even at the last minute to slow the rapid advance of AI and keep us from becoming a biological-technological hybridity. Even more unfortunate is to hear pastoral and spiritual colleagues remark, somewhat tongue in cheek but not entirely, that they do not have to worry about the inevitable and more complete rise of AI, as they gladly will not live to see the day. But our children and their children and surely their children will, which makes not looking the other way a supreme act of generativity and stewardship. If we are to be wise guardians and stewards of the future of life, pre-apprehending the divine presence of God at work in this pivotal and unprecedented moment, we will need to be diligent about meeting our clients and congregants, including the digital natives and the next generation(s) where they are in the midst of this rapidly evolving digital world. We must understand full well that they need for us not to look away but rather to help them and ourselves develop a healthy balance of attentional focus, relational skills, and technological intelligence.

THE CAPACITY TO ATTEND

Whatever our therapeutic orientation as clinical practitioners, or the therapeutic framework that helps guide and inform our practice of pastoral and spiritual care, it will be increasingly important in a digital world for us to also add to our "toolkit" a mindfulness-based approach, for there is no other therapeutic modality that focuses quite the same on helping those in our care build up their "attention muscle." Thus, even if we consider ourselves primarily psychoanalytic, family systems, or cognitive behavioral (CBT) in our orientation, just to name a few of the many therapies at our disposal, in order to be an effective practitioner in a digital age we will also need to be guided by a framework and approach that helps clients and congregants develop attentional focus and stability. Besides, the day of being a "disciple" of only one theorist and his or her approach has come and gone, for as we know now human life and development and spirituality are far too rich and complex to be captured by any single psychological, therapeutic, and theological perspective, no matter how important and compelling. And, human life and development are about to get even more complex, as we move further into the uncharted digital landscape and continue the merger with machine intelligence. To be sure, we need an informed framework that helps us address very precisely the fundamental issues of this unprecedented age, perhaps none more fundamental than preserving and enhancing the human attentional capacity. For if it goes, and there is already indication that it is shrinking, then what we value most about our human identity and spirituality, our capacity for empathy, compassion, relational intelligence, and introspective reflection will go with it. We will not in other words be human the way we have been human before, at least not in any appreciable way resembling human identity before the world of the Internet.

But there is still a moment of time and opportunity before us to say, using Michael Harris' word, "Wait!," doing all we can as pastoral and spiritual care providers and as therapy and mental health practitioners to take full advantage of the moment, helping those in our care learn to develop attentional focus. It will not come naturally, given the brain's predisposition for attentional breadth over depth and the way the digital culture is feeding this neural inclination. However, in the context of mindfulness-based therapy and mindfulness-informed pastoral and spiritual care, we can help clients and congregants learn to "downshift," as they work to develop both during and outside the therapy session a more focused attention. Over time, there can be an enhanced capacity for attentional control and mindful awareness, "knowing that you are experiencing what you are experiencing—including preconceptual awareness of fluctuations in the field of awareness" (Morgan *et al.*, 2013, p. 80). The importance of this for pastoral, spiritual, and therapeutic practice cannot be overstated, for the *digital* fluctuations in our field of awareness, the many alerts, updates, messages, pop-ups, and "breaking news" are multiplying exponentially.

We know that too much stimulation "interferes with optimal presence," so that "performance increases up to a certain point of arousal, and thereafter drops as arousal continues to increase" (Morgan, *et al.*, 2013, p. 81). As the Iowa State study revealed, video gamers have no problem with "presence" and with attentional control *as long as* they are on the screen, getting a steady dopamine "whoosh" from the gaming. But, when they are not gaming, when they return to ordinary and mundane real-world living, to the world of inter- and intrapersonal human relations, "performance" in the form of attentional stability and sustained concentration drops off precipitously. If we are to hold on to the things we value most about our humanity, then all of us, not only digital natives and gamers but also digital immigrants too, will need to strengthen our attentional capacity for both life on *and off* the screen. As David Levy (2016) has noted in *Mindful Tech*, in a rapidly accelerating digital world, "attention is the key," and more precisely what we would call task-focus attention: "The ability to remain focused on whatever you are doing at the moment," again both on and off the screen, and to "maintain that focus in the face of the seemingly endless opportunities to wander somewhere else" (p. 4).This would include, for example, maintaining our relational focus with a friend, loved one, colleague, with self and with God, when in the back of our mind we know the electronic screen is calling us to resume the video game, to check the social media alerts, to not miss out on the latest breaking news.

In the context of mindfulness practice in general and more specifically mindfulness-based care and therapy, "the goal here is to calm the mind, and to teach it to stay a particular course for a period of time, thus practicing concentration and sustained attention" (Verhaeghen, 2017, p. 7). This is facilitated over time by the regular practice of mindfulness meditation and/or contemplative prayer, depending on one's religious or spiritual orientation, both during the therapy session with a skilled practitioner and perhaps even more importantly between sessions, self-directed and with others in a contemplative-meditational group. If in time the practice becomes more transformational as a way of life, helping us shift from the busy doing mode of mind to a more contemplative mode, "you ultimately learn to be where you are" (Verhaeghen, 2017, p. 7). Put more spiritually, we learn to be centered in the gift of the present moment, even with the rush of digital fluctuations. But, this contemplative re-orientation will not come naturally, given the brain's predisposition to be very focused on the totality rather than the depth of stimuli, anticipating the potential future impact any and all of it might have on us. With the neuroscientific research and findings always in mind, the mindfulness-based care provider will therefore introduce clients to contemplative-meditational practices that foster one-pointed concentration, which over time build up and strengthen one's attentional capacity. "In focused-attention meditation, the meditator focuses (or tries to focus) on a single object, unwaveringly and clearly," often the *breath* for those just beginning meditational practice. (Verhaeghen, 2017, p. 7). In other cases, the attention "anchor" could very well be a contemplative word or mantra for those learning the practice of the Christian Centering Prayer, another form of single-pointed concentration when viewed from the standpoint of neuroscience. Or a combination of any of these, today focusing one's attention on the breath, tomorrow focusing on a sacred word of Scripture or a spiritual mantra that elicits a deep resonance.

In any case, it is important to help those in our care understand that focused-attention meditation, in whatever shape and form, will not always come naturally given the brain's focus on breadth, which in a world lived increasingly on the screen would be in the form of unrelenting digital fluctuations. There will be times and particular days, even for experienced meditators and contemplative practitioners, when the mental chatter and distractions do not seem to let up. In those moments of spiritual practice, we simply return, as Thomas Keating (2006) encourages, ever so gently to our attentional anchor, and the operative words for him are *ever so*. Focused-attention meditation, in any of the forms, consists of observing, mindfully, the distractions and intrusions and fluctuations that enter the mind, without reacting to or needing to do anything about them, other than ever so gently letting them come and more importantly letting them go. We learn to return again and again to the object of concentration, that which anchors our attentional focus, in the case of mindfulness practice it would be the breath:

> This, it turns out, is hard: The mind starts to wander, sudden itches and twitches and aches pop up and vie for attention, sleepiness creeps in—all sorts of distraction or dullness appear. When this happens, you simply notice them and go calmly back to the breath—over and over again, without judging, without reacting. (Verhaeghen, 2017, p. 7)

If we intend as pastoral and spiritual care providers, psychotherapists, and mental health practitioners to help our clients and congregants effectively develop greater attentional focus and stability in the midst of a digital age, by way of regular mindfulness and/or contemplative spiritual practice, we will need to be sure that first and foremost this is something we are doing for ourselves. Earlier we noted a fundamental principle that has broad application across the board for any and all practitioners, caregivers, even educators: we can only help accompany our congregants, clients, patients, and students as far as we have grown in our own personal and professional development, in this case as far as we are developing the capacity for attentional focus and mindful awareness in our own meditational or contemplative spiritual practice. "One of the main benefits of developing *our own* (italics mine) meditation practice is that it helps us gain confidence in using mindfulness under a variety of circumstances and with different states of mind," so that "this personal understanding and knowledge can guide and facilitate skillful interventions with [those in our care]" (Pollak, 2013, p. 135). As we have seen, for Christian practitioners the Centering Prayer method is an excellent starting point in terms of a contemplative resource that simultaneously facilitates spiritual growth *and* attentional focus, for ourselves and then in our work with clients and congregants. Additionally, we were introduced to the compassion-meditation practice, which has the capacity to increase our relational awareness and compassionate behavior toward self and others by reducing mind wandering. And now, in this final chapter it is also worth including the focused-attention meditation, a mindfulness practice that is designed to help us build up over time our attentional capacity, as we learn to more effectively monitor and regulate external and internal stimuli:

> Find a comfortable position. Close your eyes. Allow your body to be held, supported by the chair. Notice directly the sensation of your body in contact with the chair.

Take two or three slow, deep breaths, relaxing with the exhalation. With each exhalation, imagine the body becoming heavier and relaxing more fully.

Allow the breath to find its natural, easy rhythm. Enjoy the relaxed simplicity of sitting and breathing.

Where do you notice the flow of sensations of the breath most vividly—at the nose tip, the throat, the chest, or the diaphragm? Allow the attention to alight there easily, like a bird on a branch or cork bobbing on the surface of the ocean.

Whenever your attention wanders, and you notice that it has wandered, first reestablish the relaxed breath, then return your attention to the flowing sensations of breath where they are strongest.

Allow yourself a few more breaths before slowly opening the eyes. (Morgan, *et al.*, 2013, pp. 82–83)

It is interesting that attention to the rhythm of the breath, a fundamental feature of mindfulness meditation as well as focused-attention meditation, has resonance with Ignatius' (1991) approach to contemplative prayer, specifically the "Three Methods of Praying:" identify the subject manner of contemplative prayer, which like the Centering Prayer method could be a sacred word or mantra; meditate on the deeper meaning of the word or mantra; and repeat it "according to rhythmic measures" (pp. 178–182). We can probably assume that Ignatius (1991) did not have in mind building up the attentional capacity of contemplative practitioners, or maybe he did along with deepening our spiritual experience of God, and yet either way meditating or praying in "rhythmic measures" with the breath will above and beyond the spiritual benefits strengthen the attentional circuitry in the brain. All of the contemplative-meditational methods that we have identified in this book, and there are many others, whether mindfulness-based and/or more spiritually contemplative in nature, share a common feature when viewed from the standpoint of neuroscience: they enhance our capacity for attentional depth, whether this is their primary intention or not, a matter of increasing importance if we hope to hold on to and preserve what we value most about our humanity. As human beings, we still possess a "characteristic capacity for attention," and yet in uniquely powerful and unprecedented ways "our environments are active too, calling our attention to features within them, imposing themselves upon us" (Ganeri, 2018, p. 9). And the digital environment in which we find ourselves located at present and for the foreseeable future will only become more and more active, calling our attention to the incessant flow of data and information on the screen, challenging our attentional *as well as* relational and spiritual capacities like never before.

Already, our brain is habituating, or at least trying to habituate to the world of digital technologies, the amazing adaptation machine that it is, but there are signs, e.g., a shrinking attentional capacity, that even now when we are *only* in the stage of artificial narrow intelligence (ANI) that it is beginning to function on overload. Still, there is a moment of time and opportunity before us, which given the rapid acceleration and proliferation of the technologies we will likely never have again. It is a moment to say "Wait!" in order to help guide the process forward in loving and compassionate ways, a moment to preserve something of the precious quality of human consciousness and other social and relational qualities unique to our humanity, even as we continue to grow in technological intelligence. But this necessarily presupposes that we will have been able to sustain the capacity for attentional focus and control, both as individuals and collectively as a human society. For the human capacity for attention is ultimately "situated in a social world with others," which makes the human quality of empathy for example "a distinct kind of attention, attention through embodied comportment to the feelings, commitments, and wishes of others as others" (Ganeri, 2018, pp. 3–4). To be human is to attend, not only to the digital screen that is ever before us, but also with mindful awareness and compassion to the deeper reality of one's existence and the existence of others, and to the reality of divine presence at work even in this unprecedented moment. We do well not to let the moment slip away:

> Attention is the selective placing and focal accessing that brings a world to view and provides orientation within it. The attentional structure of consciousness itself explains how we are situated in a world and how we have reasons for what we do and think. To be conscious in the world is, moreover, to be able to project oneself into its past and future; it is to be able to view the world including oneself from the perspectives of conscious others; and it is to understand one's finitude and flow and the fluid boundaries that define one. The life-blood for this range of embodied skills—skills which together constitute our common humanity—is our capacity to attend. (Ganeri, 2018, pp. 28–29)

Conclusion

At the beginning of his book, *Cyber-humans: Our future with machines*, the computer researcher and engineer, Woodrow Barfield (2015) writes:

> Let me start the book with a controversial and bold statement—our future is to merge with artificially intelligent machines . . . I do not mean to imply that in the coming decades we humans will look and act like robots on an assembly line, rather that we will be equipped with so much technology, including computing devices implanted within the brain itself, that we will have been transformed from a biological being into a technology-based being, evolving under the laws of technology more so than under the laws of biological evolution. At the same time that we are becoming more "machine like" (or "cyborg like"), advances in robotics, artificial intelligence, neuroscience, and materials engineering are allowing scientists to create intelligent machines that have sophisticated human-like functionality and are rapidly gaining in intelligence—"they" are becoming like us. I see the logical outcome of technological advancements in robotics, artificial intelligence, prosthesis, and brain implants, as a future merger between humans and machines. This will not be a conscious decision made by humanity, but will be a gradual process, and inevitable. But not so gradual as to take centuries, but in all likelihood something that will happen this century or early next. As a confession, I may have played a small role in this outcome (our future merger with machines), because as a faculty in engineering, I headed a research laboratory whose goal was to design wearable computing and sensor technology that was fully integrated with the human body. . . . At the time, my colleagues and I also mused about the future directions of "wearable" devices, making predictions about technology that are being implemented today. But, in hindsight, it seems that we did not go far enough predicting the future that has unfolded and we were too conservative in stating how close we are to the Singularity and afterwards Posthuman age. (p. 1)

This is a rather bold and audacious statement, and yet it is hardly empty speculation when we stop to consider the *speed* with which machine intelligence is evolving, as we discussed in chapter 1. James Hendler and Alice Mulvehill (2016), for example, working on the "front lines" of machine learning, noted that as they were writing the first draft of the book, *Social Machines*, the consensus among computer scientists was that it would be very difficult for an AI system to beat a human anytime soon at the complicated Chinese board game of Go, let alone the reigning world champion. But as they were editing the manuscript for final submission, they had to update that chapter of the book to say that digital technologies were making it possible for a computer to reach human-level play. Nor was that all: before they ever got the page proofs from the publisher, they were rewriting the chapter again to talk about AlphaGo's stunning victory over several of the best human players in the world. And, if the book had still been in the production process a year after its publication, they would have needed yet another update, announcing that in 2017 it had defeated the top-ranked player in the world. Similarly, as I put the finishing touches on my own manuscript, I have discovered that AlphaGo, Google's DeepMind AI program, has in a few short years already become obsolete, having been supplanted by an even more powerful program, AlphaGo Zero. What is the difference? Whereas AlphaGo, notwithstanding its remarkable prowess, relied mostly on *human* programmers and players to build up its knowledge base of the game, AlphaGo Zero is self-taught and therefore self-reliant, learning on its own from a blank slate. "Whereas AlphaGo took months to get to the point where it could take on a professional, AlphaGo Zero got there in just three days, using a fraction of the processing power" (Cellan-Jones, 2017). Indeed, it performed at a superhuman level with the game of Go, along with other complicated board games, such as the Japanese version of chess, Shogi. In terms of Go, "in a game where there are more possible legal board positions than there are atoms in the universe, it was a triumph for machine over man and one that came much earlier than many in the AI world had expected" (Cellan-Jones, 2017). Once again, it is the *speed* with which machine intelligence is evolving that is taking even the AI researchers themselves by surprise, and in the case of AlphaGo Zero the rapid advance in evolution is now its own doing. "Whereas earlier versions quickly learned from and improved upon human strategies, AlphaGo Zero developed techniques which the professional player who advised DeepMind said he had never seen before" (Cellan-Jones, 2017).

It is a development that some of us may find exciting, others of us a bit unsettling if not scary, "that in just a few days a machine has surpassed the knowledge of [the game of Go] acquired by humanity over thousands of years" (Cellan-Jones, 2017). The world of digital technologies and artificial intelligence, as Susan Greenfield (2015) put it so well in chapter 2, is nothing short of an "unprecedented and complex cocktail" of *both* existential opportunity *and* existential risk. In fact, we are already beginning to see narratives of theological reflection emerge around the themes of opportunity and risk, of hope and apprehension, and some that take the middle path of holding both sides of the issue in dialectical tension, as I have tried to do with this book. It is startling to hear a respected theologian of renown like Ilia Delio suggest that we have entered into an in-between phase of human evolution, that we can no longer consider ourselves pure Homo sapiens anymore, but rather at the moment "metaphoric cyborgs" on the way to becoming something more like Techno sapiens. This is another bold statement, but again like with Barfield it is not empty speculation or merely theological reflection in the abstract. Instead, this particular view reflects a clear interdisciplinary grounding in the knowledge of faith and theology *and* in the knowledge of science and technology, a mature theological stance that can hold sacred Scripture in one hand and the *Scientific American* in the other, without becoming reductionistic in either direction. Moreover, it is a theological approach to the digital age that is guided by Karl Rahner's (1978) theology of *Vorgriff*, a preapprehension of what ultimately lies ahead even if we only, as the apostle has said, see in a mirror dimly or through a glass darkly (I Corinthians 13:12). What we do not know about life, the universe, and God is vastly greater than what we do know, as we have been learning from the contemporary sciences: astrophysics, quantum mechanics, subatomic theory, and of course the field of deep machine learning. Rahner offers us a theological framework, Ignatian to be sure, that can help us develop an openness for finding God in all things, even in the inorganic world of computer science and artificial intelligence. For God, in the words of the prophet, is always and forever doing a new thing in the world (Isaiah 43:19), so who can ever say definitively that God is not somehow and in some way in the details of our growing merger with machines. What is more immediate is how we as stewards and guardians of the future will be helping to guide the evolutionary process forward, which is now driven with increasing speed and power by technology. Do we intend to help guide the process forward in loving and compassionate ways, making good use of the digital technologies with all people in mind, or will the process be driven more by profit and greed, which once again makes it more of a *human* issue or problem than anything?

If we are in fact approaching a significant tipping point in human history and more fundamentally in human evolution, then there is a sense of urgency that we develop sooner rather than later a more coherent and in-depth theology of technology, more specifically a pastoral and practical theology that takes very seriously both the unprecedented existential risk *and* existential opportunity of the present moment, as well as the hopes and fears it engenders in the hearts and minds of those in our care. We are becomingly increasingly "borged," to use Delio's (2008) word, as we spend more of our lives on the screen, as we cede more of the everyday decision-making to machine intelligence and to our digital assistants, and as we continue to be "upgraded" by way of technological enhancement and modification. The issue of what constitutes human identity and human nature in an age of technological enhancement, and whether technologically enhanced human beings, not to mention Techno sapiens are still a reflection of *imago Dei*, must therefore become more of a central focus in our theological reflection, as we discussed in chapter 3. Barfield (2015) makes clear that even with the dramatic advances in technological enhancement that we have already witnessed *and* experienced, we have not seen anything yet, compared to what is coming our way in future years and decades. It is nothing short of a more complete merger of human beings with machines, of us becoming so "borged" that we will ultimately be a biological-technological hybridity. For some of us, this will be more challenging to get our minds around than for others, particularly if we embrace a theology of God, humanity, and creation that is more or less fixed, static, unchanging. And, while we can certainly find theological and liturgical justification for such a worldview, once again the findings of the various branches of contemporary science have revealed a universe that is anything but static and unchanging, which in my estimation is a reflection of *dynamic* divine presence. For example, there is an emerging consensus in the field of astrophysics that there may very well be more than one universe, more than our own, multiple universes within a multiverse. Perhaps the universe, life, human beings still have a long way to go after all on the scale of increasing complexity, so much so that we do well not to cling too rigidly to any theology that is overly biocentric and/or anthropomorphic in nature.

And yet, there is still a window before us, a moment to hold on to our humanity as best we can and to what we value most about it, which as we saw in chapter 4 is for Nick Bostrom (2016) the essential task of our age. The implication is that it is *not* a given, our humanity, at least not in its present shape and form, even if certain theological and liturgical constructs suggest that it is nothing short of eternal in nature. But this theological framework, rooted in the vestiges of a Western paradigm that views life and reality as more fixed and static, stands in urgent need of reframing, in light of what we are learning about the truly dynamic nature of life, including our own human life. Already we are in the midst of an evolutionary transition as "metaphoric cyborgs," somewhere between Homo sapiens and Techno sapiens, on our way to becoming more of a biological-technological hybridity. And the transition will be even more pronounced if not dramatic, as it becomes less of a metaphorical and more of a literal reality. There is, however, another important dimension to human experience that we do not want to overlook, above and beyond biology and technology, namely human spirituality. Holding on to our humanity is at bottom a spiritual endeavor, for the qualities we most want to preserve, our compassion and empathy, our introspective processing and reflection, our relational intelligence and "people skills, are fundamentally *spiritual* qualities that ground our existence. It is therefore more of a threefold hybridity that we will be working toward as pastoral and spiritual care providers, as pastoral and practical theologians: biological, technological, *and* spiritual. But to preserve the most precious qualities of human identity and spirituality assumes that we will be able to hold on to something even more fundamental, the human attentional capacity, for if it were to erode, and there is already some indication that it has started to decline, then by default the digital technologies will determine for us who we become based on *our* online usage and habits. And as we have seen, this may not always be in our best interests, in the interest of our spiritual growth and development. For example, as we spend more and more time on the screen, in the world of social media and social networking, compelled by the fear of missing out (FOMO) and/or by the need for social comparison, studies are revealing that our empathy is declining too, most pronounced in the form of cyberbullying and online cruelty.

The issue for pastoral and spiritual care providers, and by extension for clinical and mental health practitioners, is the preservation of the human attentional capacity, a matter of some urgency in a digital age. Without it, we cannot realistically expect to hold on to our humanity, to preserve the qualities we value most about human identity and spirituality. But how to preserve, not to mention enhance our attentional focus, when at every turn the digital culture is seemingly working against it? We learned in chapter 5 that the emerging field of contemplative neuroscience offers us a way forward, with research revealing that the regular practice of contemplative prayer and/or mindfulness meditation strengthens over time the neural circuitry of attention along with the circuitry associated with higher-order executive functioning, while at the same time lowering activity in the stress region of the brain. It amounts to "rigging" our own neurological system as it were, if we use Harari's (2017) word. The human brain after all is not predisposed toward attentional depth and control, but rather to as much attentional breadth as possible, in the interests of our evolutionary survival. Calming and focusing the anxious brain in other words does not come naturally, nor does letting go of our worry about tomorrow. If Jesus were teaching in today's frenetic digital world, I would think that his message would be contextualized accordingly: Along with encouraging us not to worry about *tomorrow*, he would also be urging us not to worry about the next *moment*. As we move further and further into the digital age, we and those in our care will need specific contemplative-meditational practices that build up our "attention muscle," and our capacity for empathic, compassionate, and relational awareness. We were introduced to the practice of compassion meditation and to the contemplative practice of the Christian Centering Prayer, methods that above and beyond the spiritual benefits of bringing us closer to God can and do foster attentional control by reducing mind wandering. It is more than a little ironic that Christian pastoral and spiritual practitioners even need to have this conversation in the first place, even need the findings of neuroscience to give us a nudge when the church already has a rich historical tradition of contemplative practice. But alas we do, for contemplative theology and spirituality in more recent years has too often been relegated to the periphery in the context of the Western church, which is why I am arguing for its immediate elevation to a place of comparable importance with belief and doctrine. This reflects not only an awareness of the need for preserving the human attentional capacity, but also a clear understanding of the emerging "contemplative-meditational religion" embraced by digital natives, perhaps already an irreversible trend in keeping with Rahner's (1971) observation that in the future, *now* in fact, we will become a mystic or nothing at all.

Finally, we discovered that mindfulness-based therapeutic approaches, for example Mindfulness-Based Cognitive Therapy (MBCT), intentionally focus on building up attentional stability and mindful awareness, more so than any other therapeutic modality. They therefore offer a useful framework for developing a pastoral- and spiritual-care approach that is mindfulness-informed, that reflects a clear understanding of what is at stake for human life and experience in a digital age. The human brain has long been predisposed for keeping us vigilant and active, which ultimately favors the busy doing mode, and more so now as it tries to process the tsunami of digital information. But there is still a way for us to periodically disengage from the tsunami, even with the accelerating speed of digital technologies and artificial intelligence, a way for us to calm and steady the mind by shifting from the automatic-pilot mode of doing to the more contemplative mode of being, resting in a deep awareness of the gift of the present moment and the gift of divine presence. In learning to decenter from our anxious thoughts of missing out on some important piece of digital information, and how we compare to this person or group of persons in the world of social media, we are literally reducing the turbulence in our own mind and brain. We learn that we do not have to *do* anything with the anxious thoughts and feelings, with the torrent of digital fluctuations other than to *be* mindfully aware of them, letting them come and more importantly letting them go, as we create for ourselves a sense of emotional and spiritual balance and attunement. This we learn by way of a regular mindfulness and/or contemplative spiritual practice, such as the Centering Prayer method or as we found in chapter six the focused-attention meditation, among many other contemplative-meditational approaches. The regular centering or mindfulness practice can and will strengthen the attentional circuitry in the brain of clients and congregants, in our own brain too as we develop a regular spiritual practice for ourselves. Over time, this has the potential to become a more contemplative if not transformational way of life. In a digital age, we will necessarily have to work on building up our technological intelligence in order to function and flourish, otherwise the train that is about to depart the station will soon leave us far behind. At the same time, if we hope to hold on to the most precious qualities of human existence, what has made us uniquely human for so long, we will need to preserve and fortify our capacity for focused attention. For the capacity to attend with depth and centeredness, with empathy and compassion, with good-humored decency is indeed the lifeblood for our common humanity.

References

Aharonov, D. & Vazirani, U. (2013). Is quantum mechanics falsifiable? A computational perspective on the foundations of quantum mechanics. In B. J. Copeland, C. J. Posey, & O. Shagrir (Eds.), *Computability: Turing, Gödel, Church, and beyond* (pp. 329–350). Cambridge, MA: MIT Press.

Augé, M. (1995). *Non-places: Introduction to an anthropology of supermodernity.* J. Howe (Trans.). London: Verso.

Bailey, K., West, R., & Anderson, C.A. (2010). A negative association between video game experience and proactive cognitive control. *Psychophysiology, 47 (1)*, 34–42. doi: 10.1111/j.1469–8986.2009.00925.x.

Barbour, I. (1992). *Ethics in an age of technology: The Gifford Lectures 1989–1991* (Vol. 2). San Francisco: HarperCollins.

Barbour, I. (1997). *Religion and science: Historical and contemporary issues.* San Francisco: Harper.

Barfield, W. (2015). *Cyber-humans: Our future with machines.* Heidelberg, Germany: Springer (Copernicus).

Beauregard, M. (2012). *Brain wars: The scientific battle over the existence of the mind and the proof that will change the way we live our lives.* San Francisco: HarperOne.

Bermúdez, J.P. (2017). Social media and self-control: The vices and virtues of attention. In C.G. Prado (Ed.), *Social media and your brain: Web-based communication is changing how we think and express ourselves* (pp. 57–74). Santa Barbara, CA: Praeger.

Bernstein, L. (2017, April 4). 20 percent of patients with serious conditions are first misdiagnosed, study says. *The Washington Post.* Retrieved from http://www.washingtonpost.com.

Bigdoli, H. (2017). *Management information systems* (7th ed.). Boston, MA: Cengage.

Bingaman, K. A. (2014). *The power of neuroplasticity for pastoral and spiritual care.* Lanham, MD: Lexington Books.

Bostrom, N. (2016). *Superintelligence: Paths, dangers, and strategies.* Oxford, UK: Oxford University.

Bourgeault, C. (2016). *The heart of Centering Prayer: Nondual Christianity in theory and practice.* Boulder, CO: Shambhala.

Carr, N. (2010). *The shallows: What the Internet is doing to our brains.* New York: W.W. Norton.

Ceballos, G., Ehrlich, P. & Dirzo, R. (2017). Biological annihilation via the ongoing sixth mass extinction signaled by vertebrate population losses and declines. *Proceedings of the National Academy of Sciences of the United States of America, 114 (30)*, E6089–E6096.

Cellan-Jones, R. (2017, October 18). Google DeepMind: AI becomes more alien. *BBC News.* Retrieved from https://www.bbc.com/news/technology-4166870.

Coffman, S.J., Dimidjian, S., & Baer, R.A. (2006). Mindfulness-based cognitive therapy for prevention of depressive relapse. In R.A. Baer (Ed.), *Mindfulness-based treatment approaches* (pp. 31–50). New York: Academic Press.

Cole-Turner, R. (2000). Science, technology, and mission. In M. Stackhouse, T. Dearborn, & S. Paeth (Eds.), *The local church in a global era: Reflections for a new century* (pp. 100–112). Eugene, OR: Wipf & Stock.

Cole-Turner, R. (2011a). The transhumanist challenge. In R. Cole-Turner (Ed.), *Transhumanism and transcendence: Christian hope in an age of technological enhancement* (pp. 1–18). Washington, DC: Georgetown University.

Cole-Turner, R. (2011b). Transhumanism and Christianity. In R. Cole-Turner (Ed.), *Transhumanism and transcendence: Christian hope in an age of technological enhancement* (pp. 193–203). Washington, DC: Georgetown University.

Crane, R. (2017). *Mindfulness-based cognitive therapy: Distinctive features* (2nd ed.). London: Routledge.

Cyberbullying Research Center. (2016). 2016 cyberbullying data. Orlando, FL.

Davidson, R.J. (2012). *The emotional life of your brain: How its unique patterns affect the way you think, feel, and live—and how you can change them.* New York: Plume.

Dawkins, R. (1996). *River out of Eden: A Darwinian view of life.* New York: Basic.

Deane-Drummond, C. (2015). Remaking human nature: Transhumanism, theology, and creatureliness in bioethical controversies. In C. Mercer & T.J. Trothen (Eds.), *Religion and transhumanism: The unknown future of human enhancement* (pp. 245–254). Santa Barbara, CA: Praeger.

Delio, I. (2008). *Christ in evolution.* Maryknoll, NY: Orbis.

Delio, I. (2013). *The unbearable wholeness of being.* Maryknoll, NY: Orbis.

Doehring, C. (2015). *The practice of pastoral care: A postmodern approach.* Louisville, KY: Westminster John Knox.

Fisher, M. (2015). More human than the human? Toward a "transhumanist" Christian theological anthropology. In C. Mercer & T.J. Trothen (Eds.), *Religion and transhumanism: The unknown future of human enhancement* (pp. 23–38). Santa Barbara, CA: Praeger.

Fresco, D., Flynn, J., Mennin, D., & Haigh, E. (2011). Mindfulness-based cognitive therapy. In J. Herbert & E. Forman (Eds.), *Acceptance and mindfulness in cognitive behavior therapy: Understanding and applying the new therapies* (pp. 57–82). Hoboken, NJ: John Wiley.

Freud, S. (1961). *Civilization and its discontents.* J. Strachey (Ed. & Trans.). New York: W.W. Norton.

Friedman, L. (2014, April 22). IBM's Watson supercomputer may soon be the best doctor in the world. *Business Insider.* Retrieved from http://www.businessinsider.com

Ganeri, J. (2018). *Attention, not self.* New York: Oxford University.

Garner, S. (2011). The hopeful cyborg. In R. Cole-Turner (Ed.), *Transhumanism and Transcendence: Christian hope in an age of technological enhancement* (pp. 87–100). Washington, DC: Georgetown University.

Gergen, K. (2000). *The saturated self: Dilemmas of identity in contemporary life.* New York: Basic.

Germer, C.K. (2013). Mindfulness: What is it? What does it matter? In C. Germer, R. Siegel, & P. Fulton (Eds.), *Mindfulness and psychotherapy* (pp. 3–35). New York: Guilford.

Gillings, M., Hilbert, M., & Kemp, D. (2016). Information in the biosphere: Biological and digital worlds. *Trends in Ecology and Evolution, 31 (3),* 180–189.

Goleman, D. (2005). *Emotional intelligence: Why it can matter more than IQ.* New York: Bantam Books.

Green, B.P. (2015). Transhumanism and Catholic natural law: Changing human nature and changing moral norms. In C. Mercer & T.J. Trothen (Eds.), *Religion and transhumanism: The unknown future of human enhancement* (pp. 201–215). Santa Barbara, CA: Praeger.

Greenfield, S. (2015). *Mind change: How digital technologies are leaving their mark on our brains.* New York: Random House.

Hamman, J.J. (2017). *Growing down: Theology and human nature in the virtual age.* Waco, TX: Baylor University.

Harari, Y.N. (2017). *Homo Deus: A brief history of tomorrow.* New York: HarperCollins.

Harris, M. (2014). *The end of absence: Reclaiming what we have lost in a world of constant connection.* New York: Current.

Hendler, J. & Mulvehill, A. (2016). *Social machines: The coming collision of artificial intelligence, social networking, and humanity.* New York: Apress.

Herzog, W. & Maconick, R. (Producers), & Herzog, W. (Director). (2016). *Lo and behold, reveries of the connected world* [Motion Picture]. United States: Magnolia Pictures.

Hopkins, P. (2015). A salvation paradox for transhumanism: *Saving* you versus saving *you*. In C. Mercer & T.J. Trothen (Eds.), *Religion and transhumanism: The unknown future of human enhancement* (pp. 71–81). Santa Barbara, CA: Praeger.

Ignatius of Loyola. (1991). *Ignatius of Loyola: Spiritual exercises and selected works (Classics of western spirituality).* G.E. Ganss, S.J. (Ed.). New York: Paulist.

Immordino-Yang, M.H., McColl, A., Damasio, H, & Damasio, A. (2009). Neural correlates of admiration and compassion. *Proceedings of the National Academy of Sciences of the United States of America, 106 (19)*, 8021–8026.

Jazaieri, H., Lee, I.A., McGonigal, K., Jinpa, T., Doty, J.R., Gross, J.J., & Goldin, P.R. (2016). A wandering mind is a less caring mind: Daily experience sampling during compassion meditation training. *Journal of Positive Psychology, 11 (1)*, 37–50.

Kabat-Zinn, J. (2011). Some clinical applications of mindfulness meditation in medicine and psychiatry: The case of mindfulness-based stress reduction (MBSR). In J. Kabat-Zinn & R. Davidson (Eds.), *The mind's own physician: A scientific dialogue with the Dalai Lama on the healing power of meditation* (pp. 35–47). Oakland, CA: New Harbinger.

Kaku, M. (2011). *Physics of the future: How science will shape human destiny and our daily lives by the year 2100.* New York: Anchor Books.

Kaku, M. (2014). *The future of the mind: The scientific quest to understand, enhance, and empower the mind.* New York: Doubleday.

Kapleau, R.P. (1989). Quote from *Zenso Mondo* (Dialogues of the Zen masters), Trans. K. Matsuo & E. Steinhilber-Oberlin. In R.P. Kapleau (Ed.), *The three pillars of Zen: Teaching, practice, and enlightenment.* New York: Anchor.

Keating, T. (2006). *Open heart, open mind: The contemplative dimension of the gospel.* New York: Continuum.

Kegan, R. (1998). *In over our heads: The mental demands of modern life.* Cambridge, MA: Harvard University.

Kendi, I. (2017, January 21). Racial progress is real. But so is racist progress. *The New York Times.* Retrieved from http://www.nytimes.com

Kilby, K. (2004). *Karl Rahner: Theology and philosophy.* London: Routledge.

Kitroeff, N. (2016, September 25). Robots could replace 1.7 million American truckers in the next decade. *Los Angeles Times.* Retrieved from http://www.latimes.com

Klingberg, T. (2009). *The overflowing brain: Information overload and the limits of working memory.* N. Betteridge (Trans.). Oxford, UK: Oxford University.

Konrath, S.H., O'Brien, E.H., & Hsing, C. (2011). Changes in dispositional empathy in American college students over time: A meta-analysis. *Personality and Social Psychology Review, 15 (2)*, 180–198. doi: 10.1177/1088868310377395.

Kurzweil, R. (2004). The law of accelerating returns. In C. Teuscher (Ed.), *Alan Turing: Life and legacy of a great thinker* (pp. 381–416). New York: SpringerVerlag.

Lanier, J. (2017). *Dawn of the new everything: Encounters with reality and virtual reality.* New York: Henry Holt.

Lazar, S.W. (2013a). Meditation and neuroscience. In A. Fraser (Ed.), *The healing power of meditation: Leading experts on Buddhism, psychology, and medicine explore the health benefits of contemplative practice.* Boston: Shambhala.

Lazar, S.W. (2013a). The neurobiology of mindfulness. In C. Germer, R. Siegel, & P. Fulton (Eds.), *Mindfulness and psychotherapy* (pp. 282–294). New York: Guilford.

Lebacqz, K. (2011). Dignity and enhancement in the holy city. In R. Cole-Turner (Ed.), *Transhumanism and transcendence: Christian hope in an age of technological enhancement* (pp. 51–62). Washington, DC: Georgetown University.

LeDoux, J. (2002). *Synaptic self: How our brains become who we are.* New York: Viking.

Leiva, L., Böhmer, M., Gehring, S., & Krüger, A. (2012). Back to the app: The costs of mobile application interruptions. *Proceedings of the International Conference on Human-Computer Interaction with Mobile Devices and Services-Mobile HCI, Vol. 12*, 291–294. doi: 10.1145/2371574.237.1617.

Levy, D. M. (2016). *Mindful tech: How to bring balance to our digital lives.* New Haven: Yale University.

Lovelock, J. (2016). *A rough ride to the future.* New York: Overlook Press.

Ludlow, M. (2000). *Universal salvation: Eschatology in the thought of Gregory of Nyssa and Karl Rahner.* Oxford, UK: Oxford University.

Matheson, R. (2017, May 18). MIT $100K winner's optical chips perform AI computations at light speed. *MIT News.* Retrieved from news.mit.edu/

Morgan, W.D., Morgan, S.T., & Germer, C.K. (2013). Cultivating attention and compassion. In C. Germer, R. Siegel, & P. Fulton (Eds.), *Mindfulness and psychotherapy* (pp. 76–93). New York: Guilford.

Newberg, A. & Waldman, M. (2009). *How God changes your brain: Breakthrough findings from a leading neuroscientist.* New York: Ballantine.

Parker, C.B. (2015, April 22). Compassion meditation reduces "mind-wandering," Stanford research shows. *Stanford News.* Retrieved from https://news.stanford.edu/

Peters, T. (2007). Are we playing God with nanoenhancement? In F. Allhoff, P. Lin, J. Moor, & J. Weckert (Eds.), *Nanoethics: The ethical and social implications of nanotechnology* (pp. 173–183). Hoboken, NJ: Wiley-Interscience.

Pew Research Center (2014). Frequency of meditation among younger millennials. Washington, DC.

Pew Research Center. (2015, May 12). America's changing religious landscape. Washington, DC.

Pinker, S. (2007, January 29). The brain: The mystery of consciousness. *TIME.* Retrieved from time.com/

Pollak, S. (2013). Teaching mindfulness in therapy. In C. Germer, R. Siegel, & P. Fulton (Eds.), *Mindfulness and psychotherapy* (pp. 133–147). New York: Guilford.

Rahner, K. (1969). *Hearers of the word.* M. Richards (Trans.). New York: Herder & Herder.

Rahner, K. (1971). Christian living formerly and today. In *Theological investigations* (Vol. 7). D. Bourke (Trans.). London: Darton, Longman, & Todd.

Rahner, K. (1978). *Foundations of Christian faith: An introduction to the idea of Christianity.* W. Dych (Trans.). New York: Seabury.

Rahner, K. (1986). Karl Rahner at 75 years of age: Interview with Leo O'Donovan, S.J., for *America* magazine. In P. Imhof & H. Biallowons (Eds.), *Karl Rahner in dialogue: Conversations and interviews, 1965–1982* (pp. 189–197). New York: Crossroad.

Rahner, K. (1988). Science and Christian faith. In *Theological investigations* (Vol. 21). H.M. Riley (Trans.). New York: Crossroad.

Ricoeur, P. (1991). *A Ricoeur reader: Reflection and imagination.* M. Valdés (Ed.). Toronto: University of Toronto.

Roemer, L. & Orsillo, S. (2009). *Mindfulness- and acceptance-based behavioral therapies in practice.* New York: Guilford.

Rosner, J. (2016). *Healing the schism: Barth, Rosenzweig, and the new Jewish-Christian encounter.* Minneapolis: Fortress.

Schweitzer, F. (2004). *The postmodern life cycle: Challenges for church and theology.* St. Louis, MO: Chalice.

Segal, Z., Williams, M., & Teasdale, J. (2013). *Mindfulness-based cognitive therapy for depression.* New York: Guilford.

Shapiro, S.L. & Carlson, L.E. (2017). *The art and science of mindfulness: Integrating mindfulness into psychology and the helping professions* (2nd ed.). Washington, D.C.: American Psychological Association.

Sharia, M. (2015, June 9). Five futuristic baby monitors, from wearable onesies to connected booties. *Wearables.com.* Retrieved from https://www.wearables.com

Sharon, T. (2014). *Human nature in an age of biotechnology: The case for mediated posthumanism.* Dordrecht, Netherlands: Springer.

Shanahan, M. (2015). *The technological singularity*. Cambridge, MA: MIT Press.

Siegel, D. (2007). *The mindful brain: Reflection and attunement in the cultivation of well-being*. New York: W.W. Norton.

Siegel, D. (2011). *Mindsight: The new science of personal transformation*. New York: Bantam.

Small, G. & Vorgan, G. (2008). *iBrain: Surviving the technological alteration of the modern mind*. New York: HarperCollins.

Steers, M.-L., Wickham, R.E., & Acitelli, L.K. (2014). Seeing everyone else's highlight reels: How Facebook usage is linked to depressive symptoms. *Journal of Social and Clinical Psychology 33 (8)*, 701–731.

Tegmark, M. (2018). *Life 3.0: Being human in the age of artificial intelligence*. New York: Vintage.

Tillich, P. (1973). *Systematic theology: Vol. 1*. Chicago: University of Chicago.

Turkle, S. (1995). *Life on the screen: Identity in the age of the Internet*. New York: Touchstone.

Verhaeghen, P. (2017). *Presence: How mindfulness and meditation shape your brain, mind, and life*. New York: Oxford University.

Weizenbaum, J. (1976). *Computer power and human reason: From judgment to calculation*. New York: W.H. Freeman.

Weng, H.Y., Fox, A.S., Shackman, A.J., Stodola, D.E., Caldwell, J.Z.K., Olson, M.C., Rogers, G.M., & Davidson, R.J. (2013, July 1). Compassion training alters altruism and neural responses to suffering. *Psychological Science, 24 (7)*, 1171–1180.

Index

About the Author

Kirk A. Bingaman, PhD, is associate professor of Pastoral Care & Counseling at Fordham University, and a Licensed Mental Health Counselor (LMHC) in New York. His previous books include *Freud and Faith: Living in the Tension* (SUNY), *Treating the New Anxiety: A Cognitive-Theological Approach* (Jason Aronson), and *The Power of Neuroplasticity for Pastoral and Spiritual Care* (Lexington Books).